Mapping Motivation for Engagement

Employee engagement is undeniably a crucial focus point for organisations in the twenty-first century, with motivation comprising the often missing, but vital, component of the developmental mix. *Mapping Motivation for Engagement* advocates a new paradigm for the twenty-first century: away from hierarchies and command-and-control management styles, towards a bottom-up approach in which the needs and motivators of the employees take centre stage.

Co-written with Steve Jones, this is the third in a series of books that are all linked to the author James Sale's Motivational Map diagnostic tool. Each book builds on a different aspect of personal, team and organisational development. This book is a practical guide to the complexities of understanding and dealing with engagement in modern organisational life. Along with clear diagrams, reflective points, activities and a comprehensive index, the book provides free access to the online Motivational Map tool to facilitate a greater understanding of the contents. Drawing on copious amounts of the latest research, as well as models like the MacLeod Report for the UK government, this book shows how Mapping Motivation can play a significant and crucial role in making engagement a reality, instead of a dream.

Mapping Motivation for Engagement is a stimulating and thought-provoking read for a wide audience including, but not limited to, trainers and coaches working in management and motivation, experts in human resources, internal learning and development and organisational development as well as change and engagement consultants and specialists.

James Sale is the Creative Director of Motivational Maps Ltd, a training company which he co-founded in 2006, and the creator of the Motivational Maps online diagnostic tool used by over 400 consultants across 14 countries.

Steve Jones is MD of Skills for Business Training Ltd and as a result of over 20 years' experience in management and business, was invited in 2010 to serve on the Government Task Force Team looking at employee engagement, Engage for Success, which he also co-chaired for a while.

The Complete Guide to Mapping Motivation

Motivation is the fuel that powers all our endeavours, whether they be individual, team or organisational. Without motivation we are bound to achieve far less than we really could, and without motivation we will fall short of what we are truly capable of. Motivation, before the creation by James Sale of Motivational Maps, has always been a 'flaky', subjective and impressionistic topic, and so-called 'motivational speakers' are perhaps rightly not considered entirely credible. But the Motivational Map has provided both language and metrics by which motivation can now be fully understood, described and utilised effectively. The Complete Guide to Mapping Motivation provides a total overview of how motivation informs all the critical activities that we and teams and organisations undertake at work. This includes how motivation is vital to the individual on a personal level if they want to be happy and fulfilled; it includes its applications in the domains of coaching, engagement, leadership, performance appraisal, team building and organisational development and change. So much has been written in the last 30 years about behaviours that often the literature has missed the crucial point: what drives the behaviours? This new model, then, instead of trying to control behaviours, seeks to understand motivators so that everyone can reach their full potential, not via command and control, but through bottom-up collaboration and appropriate reward strategies.

The Complete Guide to Mapping Motivation is a ground-breaking, innovative and new approach to managing motivation in the workplace. As such it is an essential series of books for all leaders, managers and key personnel engaged in improving how individuals, teams and whole organisations can be more effective, productive and engaged – and how they can want all of these things too.

Mapping Motivation for Coaching
James Sale and Bevis Moynan

Mapping Motivation for Engagement
James Sale and Steve Jones

For more information about this series, please visit: www.routledge.com/The-Complete-Guide-to-Mapping-Motivation/book-series/MAPMOTIVAT

Mapping Motivation for Engagement

James Sale and Steve Jones

for the wonderful
Barbara Cox —

greetings !

Sale
14/1/20

Routledge
Taylor & Francis Group

LONDON AND NEW YORK

First published 2019
by Routledge
2 Park Square, Milton Park, Abingdon, Oxon OX14 4RN

and by Routledge
711 Third Avenue, New York, NY 10017

Routledge is an imprint of the Taylor & Francis Group, an informa business

© 2019 James Sale and Steve Jones

Cover image "Meeting of Minds" by Linda E Sale
www.linda-sale-fine-art.com lindaesale@gmail.com
Photo courtesy of the artist. Used with the artist's permission

British Library Cataloguing-in-Publication Data
A catalogue record for this book is available from the British Library

Library of Congress Cataloging-in-Publication Data
A catalog record has been requested for this book

ISBN: 978-0-815-36755-0 (hbk)
ISBN: 978-1-351-25708-4 (ebk)

Typeset in Times New Roman
by Integra Software Services Pvt. Ltd.

Dedicated to

Mark Terrell – from IiP to BP and your motivational journey

and

Kim Keogh for her unswerving support without which such achievements would not have been possible. Also to James and Linda Sale for showing faith in me on my journey. Lastly, to all my family, colleagues and friends who have contributed without realising it. Thank you all!

Contents

Figures

Preface

Mapping Motivation for Engagement is the third volume in the series, The Complete Guide to Mapping Motivation. Devotees of the series may perhaps get a sense of déjà vu in that the first book was called *Mapping Motivation* but with the subtitle *Unlocking the Key to Employee Energy and Engagement*. Haven't we, therefore, already dealt with engagement in the initial work? Gladly, not! It is true that *Mapping Motivation* does cover some aspects of the relationship between leadership, engagement and motivation, specifically in Chapter 8, but the coverage is a more general, though useful, outline of the field. Indeed, leadership alone is a wide, wide sea that needs its own separate 'map' to show how it and motivation are even more deeply connected than is commonly suspected or imagined; the next and fourth book in this series, then, will be *Mapping Motivation for Leadership*. Which leaves us now to re-consider the huge ocean of engagement; and ocean it is.

Whereas it has always been obvious that leadership is of critical importance[1] in the success of any organisation, or endeavour for that matter, engagement, and its significance has been a relatively recent phenomenon, even as a management concept. William Kahn[2] was one of the first researchers to allude to its crucial role, and it has arisen almost certainly as a failure of 'scientific management' approaches[3] that had held sway in the USA and UK for at least a century.

It is to be hoped, then, that with the advent of the new twenty-first century, there will also be a new paradigm, or perhaps shift in paradigm, away from what can only be called 'old-school' thinking and behaving, towards a more necessary and effective methodology. In one sense the creation of Motivational Maps is one aspect of this 'newness'. Our own view would be that the personality tests and tools that arose after World War 2 were generation one of the serious attempts to get inside what makes an employee tick, but they had limitations. So subsequently, generation two, a wave a psychometric tools developed that enabled a wider sweep (but which still included personality) of qualities to be assessed. But the advantage of the psychometric was its arduous validation process whereby its measures were compared to a representative sample of the population at least twice.[4] This was and is all well and good, except the net effect of it has been to disempower leadership in two ways: first, the very fact that the psychometric requires (in the second testing) for the subject to be consistent actually tends to hypostatise the person – or put another way, 'fix' or stereotype them. Which leads to the second problem: leaders, instead of employing engaging managers and able leaders based on a range of criteria – critically motivation should be one of them – tend to look for the simple and simplistic solution of the 'right' psychometric profile.[5]

And that is why Motivational Maps as a third generation tool is really the right idea at the right time, for in yet another important way it does what the other tools do not: it reverses the flow of management focus. What do we mean by that exactly? Well, personality and psychometric tools operate on a top-down approach: it invariably seems to be about finding out whether the employee fits the manager's box. Top-down or command and control[6] in other words. Motivational Maps cannot and do not work like that: the essence of doing a Motivational Map is to understand the employee in order for the management to accommodate the employee, not the other way round. In short, it is a bottom-up approach, a people-centric approach, an engagement approach. This approach, as we discuss at length in Chapter 4, opens up the employee voice and is empowering for management too, especially in the way that it does three important things: it increases productivity, it anticipates customer needs more quickly and readily, and it facilitates greater innovation. All vital in the twenty-first century economy; and, beneficially, all likely to enhance personal well-being as well as organisational profits.

This work is a standalone, although it builds on the foundation of *Mapping Motivation*,[7] the primary source book, and of *Mapping Motivation for Coaching*,[8] its sequel. We have tried to keep repetition of materials to a minimum, so that readers of this work, if they enjoy it, will definitely like the former texts and derive enormous benefit from them. To help get the reader up to speed as quickly as possible, each book in the new Complete Guide to Mapping Motivation series will contain a brief introductory and summary chapter explaining the basics of Motivational Maps; this will be distilled from *Mapping Motivation*. This overview of the Motivational Maps' structure and meaning should enable any reader to be able to understand pretty quickly what this is all about.

There are powerful ideas to be found here, as well as transformative techniques and tools to be deployed; some can be used in an isolated and one-off kind of way, others can be used in combination, and still more others require Motivational Map technology. But we are not prescriptive; on the contrary, pragmatism rules – will it work for you? If so, use it. At the end of the day we all need to understand that management and psychological models are not reality:[9] they are a map of reality, and all maps suffer from the deficiency of being incomplete to a greater or lesser extent. As it happens, Motivational Mapping, as a model, is extremely accurate,[10] and the results it produces at the individual, team and organisational level have been nothing short of astonishing and revelatory to those concerned. We hope that you, too, will enjoy a similar sense of astonishment and revelation as you read through this work – and ultimately will want to become more involved.

Underpinning it all, then, is the Motivational Map, which we give full access to in Endnote 20 of the Introduction. You may wish to go there immediately in order to activate your personal Motivational Map as a prelude to reading this book. Certainly, the contents will make even more sense to you if you do.

This leads on to one final point in this Preface: namely, that this book has not been written in a strictly sequential way, but rather topologically; it is entirely possible to dip in and out of it as one's interests dictate. Basically, we use the MacLeod Report and its four engagement enablers as the template around which we thread Map applications and what we consider to be simple but in-depth ideas that help generate more employee engagement. But as you will see, engagement – like this book – is a tapestry: there are many threads and they interconnect and interact with each other. So you will find thematic threads – especially of leadership and engaging management – continually cropping up and not only located in their specific chapters. Go ahead – read, explore, enjoy, and focus on motivation, for it will lead to engagement as you will see.

Notes

1 Indeed, almost certainly the number one factor, without which all other good things – for example, a great product, a positive culture, powerful marketing – tend to fail.
2 William A Kahn, Psychological conditions of personal engagement and disengagement at work, *Academy of Management Journal* (1990).
3 'Taylorism' as it was known: Frederick Taylor, *The Principles of Scientific Management*, Harper and Row (1911).
4 See Cindy Boisvert, https://bit.ly/2qw0ySr.
5 Lest this be thought fanciful, consider Paul Flowers, the once chair of the Co-operative Banking Group (and who nearly destroyed the bank) and who was described by the UK Government's treasury committee chairman Andrew Tyrie, as proving to be 'psychologically unbalanced but psychometrically brilliant'. For more on this see: James Sale, https://bit.ly/2H4YneP.
6 Of course, as we say about Maps more generally, context is everything: there are situations (often very high risk and dangerous) where command and control is the best way to manage a situation or event. That said, however, in modern democracies this approach for day-to-day work and business is increasingly seen as authoritarian and ineffective.
7 James Sale, *Mapping Motivation*, Gower (2016).
8 James Sale and Bevis Moynan, *Mapping Motivation for Coaching*, Routledge (2018).
9 'A map is not the territory it represents, but, if correct, it has a similar structure to the territory, which accounts for its usefulness.' – Alfred Korzybski, Science and Sanity, 1933. This expression subsequently became a major principle underpinning neuro-linguistic programming (NLP), whose application we consider in much more detail in Chapter 4 of this book.
10 For example, face validity testing – which asks users of the Motivational Map to rate its accuracy – records a 95% accuracy rating.

Acknowledgements

We would like to thank all the licensees of Motivational Maps – over 400 worldwide – and especially our senior practitioners: Bevis Moynan, Carole Gaskell, Jane Thomas, Kate Turner, Susannah Brade-Waring and Heath Waring, and Akeela Davies, who keep the flame full and burning.

We are grateful, too, for those three companies who have allowed us to use their map work as case studies in this book: Andrew Shaw erstwhile of FGH, Warren Munson of The Inspire Professional Services, and Lloyd Bates of Aish Technologies.

Also, we'd like to thank Ali Stewart and Dr Derek Biddle for permission to use their performance curve image, Figure 8.8. from Liberating Leadership, Rethink Press Ltd (2015), https://bit.ly/2HBMYGM. Also, Dorothy Westerman.

Behind the scenes James Watson and Rob Breeds have provided invaluable support and advice and we are very grateful.

Linda E Sale, the artist and managing director of Motivational Maps Ltd, has to be thanked for support and faith in the creation of this work so far reaching it cannot really be described; but what can be described is the fact that all the Figures in this book, and the cover illustration too, are her work. We are truly grateful – and in awe of her abilities.

It is important, too, that we recognise the superb work of our senior editor at Routledge, Kristina Abbotts, whose faith, confidence and help in this has been exceptional.

Introduction to Motivational Maps

Employee engagement has become a central concern of organisations over the last 30 years or so. Engagement per se seems to have begun as an organisational and managerial concept in 1990 with the work of William Kahn,[1] and since then it has spread like wild fire; that said, however, the definition of employee engagement varies from authority to authority. But, of course, it did not arise in a vacuum; that is to say, it's not the case that one minute there was no interest in engagement, and the next, following one article, the organisational world fell in love with the concept.

If we go back in time, we find that in the 1970s there was much concern with 'enriching' workers' jobs, and in the 1980s and 1990s 'empowering' workers became a buzz concept. Underpinning these ideas were two others. First, the notion of 'job satisfaction', with the ideas of researchers like Hackman and Oldman[2] who identified five core features in job differentiation,[3] which led to three positive psychological states that employees could attain: meaningfulness, responsibility (through autonomy), and results. And second, the notion of the 'psychological contract' between employees and employers. This was an idea originally developed, according to Jean-Marie Hiltrop,[4] by Chris Argyris in the 1970s. What the psychological contract did was to attempt to head off the problem identified by David Kolb when he said: 'A company staffed by "cheated" individuals who expect far more than they get is headed for trouble'.[5] Essentially, the psychological contract is, as Mullins puts it,

> a series of mutual expectations and satisfactions of needs between the individual and the organisation. It covers a range of rights, privileges, duties and obligations which are not part of a formal agreement but still have an important influence on the behaviour of people.
>
> Mullins (1995)[6]

These are all important ideas, and preliminaries to what has come to be the proper understanding of engagement. But it is important to notice some themes already becoming apparent: most notably, as we consider the connotations of words like *satisfaction*, *meaningfulness*, *psychological*, and *expectations*, we spot their subjectivity, and also their emotional resonance, which is being introduced into the work equation. We also perhaps can anticipate their diffi-culty. For, indeed, the very phrase 'psychological contract' could be construed as oxymoronic, for a contract, surely, is a legal and binding document, a document that is explicit, clear and watertight, whereas to be psychological in nature is to be ambiguous, invisible, and imprecise. And this shift in organisa-tional focus is at the heart of the shift in the world of work, and the models that we create to explain it.

Again, and briefly, as we look back over the last century we find a profound shift happening in the world of work, which reflects advances in the wider world. Perhaps most significantly, as we headed towards the end of the twentieth century, there was a widespread appreciation of two concurrent phenomena: first, that work itself had become more complex, and was becom-ing alarmingly more so with every decade that passed. This complexity mirrored changes that were happening in society generally in the West, although also taken up by other leading world economies as globalisation meant increasing interdependencies between them. Of especial force were and are the cultural and technological developments, which have also physically transformed the social and organisational landscapes. In a nutshell, one characteristic of both the cultural and the technological shifts has been communication itself – its acceleration and speed – and this has had massive implications for how we work.

Coping with this acceleration and speed, whilst on the one hand a golden opportunity, has also been a profound, and dare we say, disturbing challenge. Another way of describing this would be to point towards the shift from the Industrial Age to the Information Age, and just as the Industrial Revolution of the nineteenth century brought in its wake huge social, cultural and technologi-cal upheaval (which was physically reflected in the relative demise of the countryside as people flocked to towns and cities), so now in the Information Age we are experiencing a similar order of shift.

This leads onto, then, our second phenomenon: the failure of Taylorism,[7] or to give it its more well-known title, scientific management. Basically, this methodology sought to make work and its job roles efficient by breaking them down into prescribed behavioural activities. Efficiency was obtained by rules, procedures, compliance and supervision, and at the expense of autonomy, creativity, responsibility, and commitment. Increasingly, being efficient, even when achieved, did not mean being effective. Many began to notice that this sort of management produced a lot of bureaucracy, as well as a certain soulless impersonality. Jacob Morgan[8] ironically commented that 'Robots aren't taking jobs away from humans; it's humans who took the jobs away from robots'. In other words, we employed humans to do the work that was far better suited to a robot!

To move on, then, we need to grasp that this model of management simply wasn't working, and continues not to work as we go further into the twenty-first century and deeper into the Information Age. It's true that many organisations still use it, despite all the evidence for its failures, which we shall come to shortly. But why would they do that? We will explore this in a lot more detail in Chapter 1, but for now suffice to say that there are powerful psychological reasons why managers and leaders won't move on to a better model of management. Of prime consideration here is probably the fact that scientific management always involves command-and-control,[9] top-down styles of leadership alongside the comforting idea that 'scientific' management is rational, and so predictable: you enter *these* inputs and – as night follows day – you must get *those* outputs. In other words, quite apart from the fact that scientific management seems to have worked fairly successfully for a hundred years or so, this system – for that is what it is – gives control and certainty, and which human being does not want that?

But, and there's always a but, as we have moved from one Age to another, and one century to another, that control and that certainty has increasingly seemed fraught and less likely. The evidence is in that employee engagement is the way forward for all organisations, large and small, and that the benefits of it are too overwhelming to ignore. What is this evidence? Well, here are a few snippets:

1. The cost of employee disengagement to the economy in 2008 was between £59.4–64.7 billion[10] per annum. That is a staggering figure, and it is for the UK alone!
2. Only 29% of employees[11] were engaged in their work. Which means that 71% are not fully engaged.
3. Companies on the Glassdoor[12] Best Places to Work list outperform the overall stock market by 115%. Best places to work are, by definition, places where employees are engaged, so from a purely financial point of view engagement is surely desirable?
4. In the UK, 82% of senior managers regard disengaged employees as one of the three greatest threats facing their business.[13] In other words, engagement is a strategic issue.
5. As many as 47% of employees stay in a job they dislike for fear of having no other option.[14] In saying this we are almost raising a moral issue: do we want to be the kind of managers who preside over misery and fear?

We could go on, but what it boils down to is an observation that Jack Welch made: 'I think any company has got to find a way to engage the mind of every single employee ... What's the alternative? Wasted minds? Uninvolved people? A labour force that's angry or bored? That doesn't make sense.'[15] It doesn't make sense for it is such a waste – of potential, of people, and of resources.

And unless we do something the situation can only get worse.

Glassdoor found, counterintuitively, that employees who stay with an organisation get increasingly unhappy year by year! You'd think that as they stay, so they must be happy, but no: Glassdoor discovered that 'a one-year increase in years of experience is associated with a 0.6-point decrease in overall employee satisfaction'.[16]

Employee engagement, then, is a movement, a concept, a methodology whose rationale is to counter 'scientific management', not for the sake of being awkward or different but because scientific management is no longer working in the modern world. That means that whatever employee engagement 'is', it will almost certainly cut across or undermine some of the key presuppositions of the scientific management approach. Such presuppositions include some of the topics we mentioned earlier: command-and-control is not usually the best way to get the best out of people; rules and regulations and endless drives for efficiency are not always the most effective thing organisations can do; and at the heart of any organisation are real people who need motivating (in their souls if you will) and people are not robots.

Arie De Geus observed that 'Organisations need profits in the same way as any living being needs oxygen. It is a necessity to stay alive, but it is not the purpose of life.'[17] This is an important observation because it points to both where organisations need to go and to where they have been. Where they have been is in the extremely limiting position of making profits the be-all and end-all of organisational existence, and so to that end, people have been subordinated and, effectively, enslaved. In a bizarre way this enslavement also includes people at the top end of the management hierarchies where the increase in plutocracy and rampant greed is all too documented: and this greed is completely divorced from performance, productivity, and any form of long-term success. Bowles and Cooper's book[18] documents in staggering detail just how serious the problem is: 'Bailouts and bonuses sent unimaginable sums of the taxpayers' money to the very people who brought calamity upon the rest of us'.

Engagement, then, first and foremost, recognises that organisations and businesses are about people first, and profits second, but it recognises as well that engaging people actually leads to greater profitability, and – as an extra bonus – greater organisational longevity too. Two metaphors may help clarify this issue. The first is a much quoted one: what is the primary purpose of a business? To make a profit? No – that is the consequence of the primary purpose. The primary purpose is to find and retain a customer; and when we do that, we end up making a profit. In other words, profitability directly assayed can be counter-productive, but indirectly approached can be much more effective. So the second metaphor that reinforces this idea is that of Tai Chi: Tai Chi moves are such that one never 'directly' strikes the enemy; indeed, all moves are circular or curved (not straight or direct in other words), and to defeat the enemy is not to strike them but to allow the enemy's own move or momentum to count against them. In other words, to achieve victory by not focussing directly on victory and what *you* are doing, but on what the other person is doing. This, of course, is slower to do, slower to learn, and seems riskier, but is actually more powerful, more assured, and ultimately more satisfying. And this is what management should be doing: not focusing on 'me' and their self-importance, but on their employees, and their 'moves', which will allow victory.

So it is no longer good enough to run an organisation as a sort of cultural and communicative apartheid whereby people at the top know everything, and people below do what they're told, for this will – as it did in the past – simply generate profits. In terms of effectiveness, this no longer works; but even in terms of efficiency it 'sucks' as well, because the complexity that we are now dealing with at organisational level is such that the withholding of information at the top can have catastrophic consequences for the employees and their relationship with the organisation, and for the organisation itself.

And when we talk about withholding information, we are not just talking about the lower or middle level stuff – operational, sales, marketing, technical, health and safety, compliance, customer information, for example – but profoundly top end material too. De Geus uses a key word in our quotation from him: *purpose*. What is our purpose? The organisation has one, but so do individuals – each individual who makes up the organisation. How do their purposes and the organisations cohere or synchronise? Is anyone thinking about this? And what about values – another important word? Or vision or mission? And do people really 'get' their organisational goals and are they aligned with some of these other words, and with their own purposes?

Already, surely, we can begin to see complexity in these questions, but necessity also: we have to get to the root of them if the organisation is to succeed and people are to thrive. Clearly, from what has been said so far, one key value of engagement has to be collaboration: that the people within an organisation have to collaborate, to share, to draw upon each other's strengths, if there is going to be the remotest chance of succeeding, of staying in business, of outperforming the competition – of which there seems to be no end. Being collaborative almost implies being more egalitarian; in short, employee engagement is partly an extension of the democratic franchise!

So we come to asking what employee engagement is, and we have already said that there are various authorities on this topic. This book is not an academic treatise in which we are going to analyse all the fine distinctions between all the varying models and then say this one is right one! Our approach has always been pragmatic: does it work in the real world? Are organisations benefitting from a specific model of engagement? What results have actually been achieved? Models, as neuro-linguistic programming (NLP)[19] tells us, are just a map, not the territory. As such they are approximations, and reading through the literature on this topic we are fully aware that some great consultants and writers have got some amazing results using employee engagement, but not our version of it. But to reassure the reader: our version, using the unique technology of Motivational Maps,[20] has also got some amazing results, which we will be discussing along the way and specifically in Chapter 9.

Key ideas surrounding engagement, however, are those of voluntary effort and going the extra mile because they want to, of commitment and trust, and of deep job satisfaction. But in all this we need to understand as well that engagement is not something that can be 'done' to employees; it is not a magic switch that we turn on, and voilà: there is the light of engagement! On the contrary, the most management can do is to create the environment in which engagement is possible, and most certain of all is the fact that without management being honest, sincere and consistent in its application of the values and principles underpinning engagement, then it is truly impossible to achieve. Thus, engagement is in essence a transformative process,[21] both for the employees and for the managers at all levels, and part of this essence takes us back to our earlier point about psychology and the way that it inevitably entails the ambiguous, the invisible, and the imprecise. Management, and leadership generally, simply has to begin to embrace the risk that comes with lack of direct control and 'controlling'.

For here's the thing (and we are going to explore a lot more about this in the following chapters): at the heart of engagement, which is a behaviour,[22] is something that is not a behaviour and without which engagement itself cannot be: namely, motivation. And the good news is, whilst we, as practitioners of motivational engagement, recognise the ambiguities, fluidities and lack of certainties that we enter into every time we encounter an organisation seeking to improve engagement, Motivational Maps actually provides statistical data that seriously reduces the risks and uncertainties that obviously accrue as one steps into these unknowns – effectively, the unknowns of the human hearts that we, and organisations the world over, are actively seeking to engage.

It is in this sort of environment, then, that we invite all managers and employees to come and grow; for that is what this involves. There will be necessarily, in the process of creating a culture of engagement, personal growth on the part of all involved; this personal growth starts with increasing self-awareness, and that means we begin with mapping motivation![23] If we can do that, if we can tap into our own motivators, which is to say our own deep psychological desires, we can avoid what Studs Terkel[24] called a 'Monday through Friday sort of dying' at work.

So, to summarise why we should research, plan and commit to creating highly engaged employees, then the benefits are plain:

1. Highly engaged employees perform better – up to 16 times better[25] – and so are more productive.
2. Highly engaged employees, therefore, increase organisational profitability or value (non-profit), and this leads to increased shareholder or stakeholder value.
3. Highly engaged employees have a superior impact on customers and clients, and so this increases satisfaction ratings as well as customer retention rates, again driving profits.
4. Highly engaged employees, because they are happier, tend to be less stressed, so less sick or late or absent, make less errors or mistakes, and stay longer, thus reducing recruitment and its associated costs and risks.

5. Highly engaged employees improve quality, because they are more focused, and ultimately contribute in a more meaningful way to the strategic direction of the organisation, since management is in a proactive two-way flow of information with them and notes what they are being told at ground level.

With these thoughts in mind, then, let's begin our journey, and we will start with the barriers to engagement and how we might overcome them. But preceding even that, you will find it useful to complete a complimentary Motivational Map which will in itself give you a clear idea of what this is about. To access how to get a Map go to Endnote 20 at the end of this section.

Notes

1 William Kahn, Psychological conditions of personal engagement and disengagement at work, *Academy of Management Journal*, Vol 33, No 4 (1990).
2 Richard Hackman and Greg Oldham, *Work Redesign*, Prentice Hall (1980).
3 Hackman and Oldham's five core features are: skill variety, task identity, task significance, autonomy, and task feedback.
4 Jean-Marie Hiltrop, The changing psychological contract: The human resource challenge of the 1990s, *European Management Journal*, Vol 13, No 3 (1995).
5 David Kolb, et al., *Organisational Psychology*, Prentice Hall (1991).
6 Laurie Mullins, *Management and Organisational Behaviour*, Pitman (1995).
7 Frederick Taylor, *The Principles of Scientific Management*, Harper and Row (1911).
8 Jacob Morgan, *The Employee Experience Advantage*, John Wiley (2017).
9 And as Kenneth Thomas points out: 'the truth was more that, under command-and-control management, workers often resisted imposed change': *Intrinsic Motivation at Work*, Berrett-Koehler (2009).
10 According to Gallup, and cited by MacLeod Report, *Engaging for Success*, Department for Business, Innovation and Skills Consultation (2009).
11 *Engaging for Success*, Department for Business, Innovation and Skills Consultation, ibid.
12 Diarmuid Russell, *Employee Engagement*, Media Planet (September 2016).
13 Hay Group, Engagement Matters, http://bit.ly/2PkrtdK (2010).
14 Research by the SHL Group, in a study of 1000 UK private and public sector employees and managers, cited in *Retail Week*, The Right Attitude, 26/11/2010, http://bit.ly/2gXkVT1.
15 Jack Welch, cited by George Langelett, *How Do I Keep My Employees Motivated?: The Practice of Empathy-Based Management*, River Grove Books (2014).
16 Mario Nunez, Does Money Buy Happiness? Glassdoor Economic Research Blog, June 18, 2015, http://bit.ly/1MtYUp0.
17 Arie De Geus, cited in Lee Bolman and Terrence Deal, *Reframing Organizations: Artistry, Choice, and Leadership*, Jossey-Bass (2004).
18 David Bowles and Cary Cooper, *The Engagement Work Culture*, Palgrave Macmillan (2012). There are some specific and fabulous examples in this book, but of particular note is the restraint of the CEO of Whole Foods who caps his CEO pay at a ratio of 19:1 with his workers compared with the US average of 300–450:1. And this in the context of some of these (300–450:1) CEOs seriously destroying value in the companies they lead: e.g. Bob Nardelli at Home Depot, Carly Fiorina at Hewlett-Packard, etc.

19 See James Sale and Bevis Moynan, *Mapping Motivation for Coaching*, Routledge (2018) for more specifically on NLP and its relationship with Motivational Mapping.

20 To obtain a link to do a complimentary Motivational Map, send an email to info@motivationalmaps.com and put the word ENGAGEMAP in the heading.

21 And what this means in essence is that to undertake 'employee engagement' is not just some feel-good exercise that we may want to implement because we are nice people, but it is a core business strategy that we can expect to deliver competitive advantage.

22 'Engagement is a behaviour' – Bowles and Cooper, op. cit. We will be expanding on this later in the book.

23 Michael Moran, CEO of 10Eighty, says,

> if you understand what is important to them, what motivates them, and what is it they like doing and consequently good at, and you sculpt their job around those three things, you will have a highly engaged, loyal and most importantly a highly productive employee which in turn will drive profitability and shareholder value.

Cited in Russell, *Employee Engagement*, op. cit. Note the requirement to understand 'what motivates them'.

24 Studs Terkel, *Working*, Ballantine (1985).

25 For more on performance and how the Pareto Principle suggests a multiple of 16 see both James Sale, *Mapping Motivation*, Routledge (2016) and James Sale and Bevis Moynan, *Mapping Motivation for Coaching*, Routledge (2018).

Summary of Motivational Maps
What you need to know in a nutshell!

Within each person there are nine motivators – we all have these motivators, and we all have the full nine; the difference is that each individual has the nine in a different order and at a different level of intensity. This gives rise to the possibility of millions of potential combinations in an individual's profile. Over 30,000 Maps have been completed and we still have never seen two individuals with identical Maps; furthermore, because motivation is partially based on our belief systems, then it changes over time. It is not static and it is not fixed, and so it is impossible to stereotype anyone according to their motivators, since these will change. Usually, most people are directly influenced not by just their top motivator, but by their top three motivators; rarely, this can be their top two or top four, but the scoring shows what really counts or not (which are motivators scoring > 20).

Motivation is energy; it is what fuels us to do 'things' – things we want to do. Without motivation we are unlikely to set out in the direction we want to go (towards our goals) and are even more unlikely to use our knowledge and skills effectively. In short, motivation is the fuel in the tank of the car we call performance. Thus, knowing what motivates us and how to reward – or re-fuel – our motivators is to enable higher levels of energy, greater levels of performance and productivity, and to seriously increase our satisfaction with life.

The nine motivators are not random or discrete; but instead form a holistic unity. They are divided into three groups of three; the groups, like the motivators themselves, have properties as well as motivational qualities. Some motivators are aligned and reinforce each other; other motivators conflict and cause tension, whether that be at an individual (that is, internal), team or organisational level. The tension is not necessarily a bad thing; it can lead, for example, to procrastination – to taking longer to make a decision – but equally taking longer can sometimes mean making a better decision. In Motivational Maps, therefore, as an absolute rule, there is no good or bad Map: context determines the meaning of every profile.

So, to expand and summarise the key principles underpinning Motivational Maps, of which there are nine:

1. All Map profiles are good. There are no good or bad profiles – the diagnostic is ipsative, which means that you are measuring yourself against yourself, so you cannot be 'wrong'. What you 'think' can be wrong but how you 'feel' cannot be: it is how you feel, and so it is with your motivation, as they are feeling based.
2. Context is everything in interpreting Maps. There can be no one meaning isolated from the context in which the individual is operating. Profiles may suit or reinforce a specific context or not; 'or not' may mean that intention (willpower), knowledge and skill will have to accomplish that which one is not motivated to do, or it can mean the difference between focus (the motivators aligned and not closely scored) and balance (the motivators less aligned and the scoring narrowing or close) and which is relevant in a given situation.
3. Motivational Maps describe, measure and monitor motivation. They make our invisible emotional drives visible and quantifiable. At last individuals, managers and organisations can get a handle on this key issue, and through reward strategies do something about it – namely, increase it. Maps are a complete language and metric of motivation.
4. Motivators change over time. This happens because our beliefs change over time and these belief changes affect how we feel and therefore what motivates us. Thus regularly monitoring of motivation is appropriate and effective. From a coaching perspective this is so powerful because it is a focused opportunity to explore, too, what one's beliefs are, and whether they are supportive of what one is trying to achieve.
5. Motivational Maps are not a psychometric instrument. Psychometric type tools inevitably describe a 'fixed' personality, a core which is unchanging. Maps are stable but fluid over time. Maps take an 'energy snapshot', for motivation is energy. Technically, Motivational Maps are a self-perception inventory.
6. Motivational Maps do not and cannot stereotype individuals. This follows from the fact they change over time, so whatever someone's profile today, there is no guarantee it will be the same tomorrow. That said, the Maps are usually stable for about 18–24 months. But nobody should suggest, in a personality sort-of-way (like saying, 'I'm an extrovert'), 'I'm a Searcher' or any other motivator.
7. There are nine motivators but they are correlated into three groups. These three groups represent, amongst other things, the three primary modes of human perception: feeling, thinking and knowing. Each perception has fascinating and differing properties.
8. Motivation is highly correlated with performance. It is possible to be a high performer and yet demotivated, but the price for this, middle- or long-term, is stress and health problems. Having a highly motivated workforce is going to reduce illness and absenteeism, as well as presenteeism (the being there in body but not in mind or spirit).

9. Motivation is a feature and people buy benefits. Let's not forget that because motivation is a feature, then it features in many core organisational (and non-organisational) activities: leadership, teams, performance, productivity, sales, appraisal, engagement (70% of engagement is motivation), recruitment, careers and more beside. People usually, therefore, buy the effect or benefit of motivation rather than wanting it directly. Think essential oils! Usually applying an essential oil to the skin requires a 'carrier' oil, and so with motivation: it's wrapping the mapping.

What, then, are the nine motivators and what do they mean (see Figure S.1)? The motivators are in an ordered sequence which correlates with Maslow's hierarchy of needs. At the base are what we call the relationship motivators (R) – representing the desire for security (the Defender), belonging (the Friend), and recognition (the Star). They are represented by the colour green, and they are relationship motivators because the primary concern of all three is people orientation.

Then, in sequence we have the three achievement (A) motivators. These are in the middle of the hierarchy. First, there is the desire for control (the Director), then the desire for money (the Builder), and finally the desire for expertise (the Expert). They are represented by the colour red, and they are achievement motivators because the primary concern of all three is work orientation.

Finally, we have the three growth (G) motivators. There are at the top of the hierarchy. These are the desire for innovation (the Creator), then the desire for autonomy (the Spirit), and at the apex – though this does not imply superiority – we have the desire for meaning or purpose (the Searcher). They are represented by the colour blue, and they are growth motivators because the primary concern of all three is self-orientation.

Figure S.1 The nine motivators

From this brief re-cap of what Motivational Maps is about we hope that – if you haven't yet encountered them directly – your first response will be: 'That's fascinating – so what is my profile? What are my top three motivators?' A good idea at this point is to request to do a Motivational Map – see Endnote 20 of the Introduction to find out how to access a Map.

Chapter 1

Barriers to engagement and productivity

In our work with organisations on implementing engagement programmes, we have used a seven step approach.

Notice that the first step (Figure 1.1) requires that we answer the question: what is employee engagement? However, before we consider what it is and how we 'get it' through the seven steps, we need to look at some preliminary barriers before we even start. These barriers are so big, so threatening, so apparently insurmountable, that unless we address them squarely and head-on, we are unlikely to make any further progress. And there are three main ones.

Activity 1.1

Write down what you think the three main barriers to employee engagement are. When you have done that compare your answers to ours. Remember, there is no absolute right or wrong here: you may have experience in an organisation or

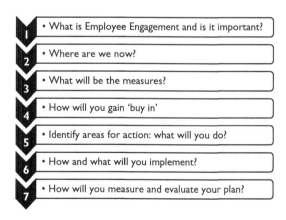

1. • What is Employee Engagement and is it important?
2. • Where are we now?
3. • What will be the measures?
4. • How will you gain 'buy in'
5. • Identify areas for action: what will you do?
6. • How and what will you implement?
7. • How will you measure and evaluate your plan?

Figure 1.1 Seven steps to employee engagement

context that entirely validates your view, but if your answers are different to ours, how do ours extend your thinking on this issue?

First, and possibly foremost, there is absolutely no point in undertaking an employee engagement programme unless there is complete buy-in from the board and Senior Management Team (SMT) of the organisation. Complete buy-in. What does this mean? It means that this is not just a Human Resources (HR) or Learning and Development (L&D) initiative; it comes from the top, is promoted by the top, and the top lead and walk the talk. If that doesn't happen, employees immediately spot the discrepancies – discrepancies between what the bosses are saying and what they are doing – and so will discount the process. Remember that engagement is about the voluntary and extra effort employees want to give the organisation because they believe in it and are truly committed. Nobody can believe in an organisation where bosses operate under one set of rules, and staff under another; it is simply self-defeating to try. Why waste organisational time and money in this way? But there is also an important implication to establish at this early stage: what does or would it mean for the board and SMT to fully embrace employee engagement? It would mean that the organisation was viewing employee engagement as a strategic imperative, not some frilly, optional extra like 'wouldn't it be nice if staff were happy?' Indeed, to be a strategic imperative means that the very existence of the organisation depends on it, and therefore that all employees, including leadership, should act on that sense of urgency. The question, then, becomes: how do we get complete buy-in? Chapters 3 and 4, and the case studies in Chapter 9, are especially relevant here.

Second, and a barrier we frequently encounter, is that of needing resources sufficient to undertake the programme. There are nine core resources to consider: money, time, equipment, people skills, knowledge, right attitude, information, space/environment and agreed co-operation (see Figure 8.11 for more on this). Any of these can be a stumbling block, but usually most can be factored into the process. But the one that comes up time and time again as being insuperable is – yes! – time. 'We simply haven't got the time to do this.' In mapping we call this 'capacity'; what is happening is that the organisation wants to 'do' engagement but they have no 'capacity', no slack in the system, to allow them the space to undertake it. Another way of putting this is to say that they are 'fully maxed'. Of course, this is counter-intuitive: how can we be fully maxed when the whole point of engagement is to enable employees to offer more? If they are 'maxed' aren't they offering all they can already? This is a great question and we will be looking at this in a lot more detail later in this chapter. But for now, suffice to say, every organisation can improve efficiencies, increase focus, avoid double-handling of tasks, and tweak systems and processes; what we are saying, in effect, is there is a lot of work being done in any organisation that is useless, pointless, and simply not productive. The mere act, therefore, of seeking to undertake an employee engagement programme begins that de-cluttering process as a necessary first step towards getting started. The question, then, becomes: how do we create the capacity to run engagement programmes? And a great starting point is, of course, to ask the employees themselves how the capacity can be created, for they more than anyone else know exactly where there are inefficiencies in the system. This has the added benefit of involving them at the start and taking them seriously.

The third barrier, surprisingly, and most intractably, is the issue of the human ego. In fact, one of the reasons why our first barrier may never be overcome – that is, we might not get complete buy-in – is because of the egos of the management and leadership. It is, if you like, the flaw in human nature that has always been there, and management writers have noted it from the beginning. Writing in the 1950s, Professor Brown talked of many leaders in British industry who were 'petty Hitlers ... working off their own mental conflicts on others to the detriment of the psychological health of the community...'[1] and more recently David Bowles[2] and Professor Cary Cooper devote an entire chapter of their engagement book to 'Ego at work'. Ego, then, is a form of total selfishness; instead of thinking about the 'we', it's all about the 'I', or 'me-first'. Instead of prioritising the mission and the welfare of the organisation, the ego is always, overtly or covertly, calculating its own self-interest – whether that be in monetary, control, expertise, or recognition terms (these are four major areas where the ego loves to lord it over others). So, the question, here, becomes: how do we obviate the negative impact of ego-driven people[3] who will almost certainly seek to derail employee engagement? There is clearly no simple solution, but in Chapters 5 and 6 we consider what it means to be an engaging manager and an effective leader, and two points to mention now are: (1) the importance of values such as honesty and transparency, and (2) the almost equal importance of the recruitment process in not appointing such ego-driven people in the first place!

As you can see, each of these three barriers has generated a further question. Keep these in mind as we move on to discuss the question: what is employee engagement?

Activity 1.2

Based upon what you have read so far, how would you define employee engagement? Make some notes about what it is and what it does.

The MacLeod Report, which is an influential UK government sponsored review of engagement best practice, commented on the fact that they had actually seen over 50 definitions of employee engagement! Furthermore, it noted that there was a danger of – and a call for[4]– the term to be abandoned altogether. Is engagement an attitude, a behaviour or an outcome? In true British spirit, the Report adopted a pragmatic approach. MacLeod says:

> We believe it is most helpful to see employee engagement as a workplace approach designed to ensure that employees are committed to their

organisation's goals and values, motivated to contribute to organisational success, and are able at the same time to enhance their own sense of well-being.

MacLeod (2009)[5]

Commitment, motivation, success and *well-being* – these are four critical words, four compass points, if you will, which will help us direct attention and focus onto improving employee engagement (Figure 1.2). And we notice that the essence of this 'approach' is win–win: the organisation is successful (and we'll look more closely at what 'success' means), and the employee experiences 'well-being'. This, then, is about co-operation – not competition – between leaders and the led, and between management and their staff; this is about a new way of working that stresses not the tangibles – cash flow, revenues, profits, equipment, data bases, offices and so on – but the invisibles: *commitment* – an attitude; *motivation* – an energy; *success* – an outcome; and *well-being* – a state. Wow! What a shift in thinking – and feeling, if it is possible to do this. And, remember, if we do, we really do, achieve this shift – then we get to the tangibles, especially the profits, tai-chi style!

But we should not underestimate the difficult of doing this, because the status quo always wants to kick back, and as the great quality guru, Philip Crosby,[6] observed: 'Good ideas and solid concepts have a great deal of difficulty in being

Figure 1.2 The four critical compass points for engagement

understood by those who earn their living by doing it some other way'. So, despite all the benefits of undertaking employee engagement, we find there is massive resistance over and above the three reasons we have already given; for the fourth barrier is simply inertial (Figure 1.3) – it's too difficult, too perilous and, besides, we are quite happy as we are, thank you. See more in Chapter 8 on resistance to change.

It should be clear from what we have said so far that however we slice the engagement cake, any part of it – as in a hologram (if we may mix metaphors) – is going to contain one central ingredient: namely, motivation. There is simply no way round this fact. Attitudes and behaviours on their own are not sufficient to create that employee 'well-being' that is the *sine qua non* of engagement. Indeed, the latter item, behaviour, is particularly fraught and problematic, for although it is a necessary feature of engagement, it is not the core; furthermore, focusing on behaviour has, potentially, an insidious consequence: basically, that we are back where we started with management 'controlling' behaviours as they have always liked to do.[7]

Motivation is the core of employee engagement, maybe, in our estimation, up to 70% of it. Why? Because it is the motivation – the invisible energy – that drives the visible behaviours. And not only that, but our attitudes too are connected with our motivators, especially commitment, which is of paramount importance in overcoming Block #1, as we shall see. Motivation is also key to unlocking what all organisations and all individuals want at a primary level. What is that?

With few exceptions[8] a key focus of employee engagement is an understanding that if employees are engaged then their performance will improve,

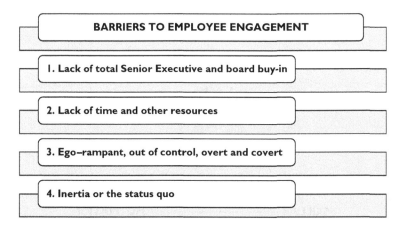

Figure 1.3 Four barriers to employee engagement

and if their performance improves, then so would their productivity. Ultimately, then, we get back to the tangibles, or what Mapping Motivation calls the 3Ps: if performances improve (individually and at team level), then this almost certainly must result in increased productivity, which – if we are producing more at no extra cost (remember that 'discretionary' and 'extra' effort the employee gives?) – must lead to greater profitability. Of course, one caveat has to be that increases in productivity do not necessarily lead to greater profits if the organisational strategy is wrong in the first place. So this neatly leads us to consider performance itself, the starting point.

Activity 1.3

What is performance? What does it mean to you? How does one improve performance in any area of your life? How important is performance to you? Why is it important? Consider these question before moving ahead.

Performance is crucial in our lives because it is, and always has been, directly correlated with rewards. That is why Mapping Motivation always talks about the appropriate reward strategies that follow anyone's, any team's, any organisation's motivational profile. We know this from childhood because when we were a 'good boy' or a 'good girl', then our parents, carers and teachers approved, applauded and ... rewarded us. In a way, not dissimilar to Pavlovian dogs, we are trained and conditioned to respond – we perform well and we anticipate those lovely rewards that make us salivate![9]

Mapping Motivation takes the view that performance is made up of three primary elements:[10] direction, skills,[11] and motivation (Figure 1.4).

Whether we are talking about an individual (employee), a team, or an organisation (or company), these three elements of performance always apply. First, we need to establish the direction we are going to go in; in employee terminology we may call this our 'career choice' – we decide 'this' or 'that'

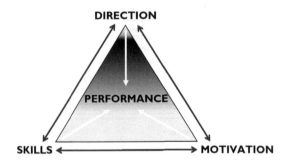

Figure 1.4 Performance pyramid

way. Similarly, teams and organisations make choices about the direction they are going in: they may call it vision, or a business plan, or goals, but whatever they are called they are absolutely mission critical. For no-one can 'win' the game of life at any level without choosing the right path[12] to walk along; and a posher word that we sometimes use in Mapping here is 'strategy'. We need an effective strategy for our organisation, otherwise we are lost; and, to be frank, no amount of motivation can compensate for going in the wrong direction. That would simply mean getting to the North Pole faster when what we wanted was to visit New York.

But lest it be thought that there is an area of life – direction/strategy – where motivation is not directly relevant, we do need to think again. For although all three separate elements are unique and distinct, if we consider them closely we find there is a motivational dimension in them all. Daniel Pink in his book, *Drive*,[13] argues that the big three intrinsic motivators are autonomy, mastery and purpose. If we think about it, what does choosing a strategy or direction essentially involve? That's right, choice, our choice. In other words, strategising, or even *not* choosing, which in itself is a choice, is some deep aspect of our desire for freedom, or autonomy, which is the 'spirit' motivator. And if we consider 'skills', we find that this very much reflects the 'expert' drive in Mapping Motivation's taxonomy. Finally, what about 'motivation' itself? This surely is our 'searcher' motivator or the desire for 'purpose', or, more exactly, meaning.[14] What motivates us is what we believe about, and how we construe the meanings of, our perceptual reality. As we are going to see, purpose from an organisational perspective is more about a moral dimension than a business one – if it is seriously going to engage employees. But the point is, although direction, skills and motivation are all discrete elements in the performance mix, underpinning them all is a motivational drive.[15]

For organisations to evolve, then, which means to progress and to improve (and this means to engage their employees) we need to consider these three elements of performance in more detail (Figure 1.5).

We see that even direction/strategy, properly considered, has a motivational intent. Which means: in whatever we do as an organisation, an underpinning principle is to motivate our employees to enable engagement. But let us consider a deeper model of performance here.

Whilst we advocate engagement as way of harnessing the full energy and wisdom of employees, it is true to say that in most situations, certainly as they currently are, staff do not get involved in organisational strategy or direction. Effectively, what this means is that we measure their performance along two axes: how skilful (and knowledgeable) they are in the execution of their tasks, and how motivated they are when they undertake them. We can write this as a simple formula:[16]

Performance (P) = Skills (S) × Motivation (M)

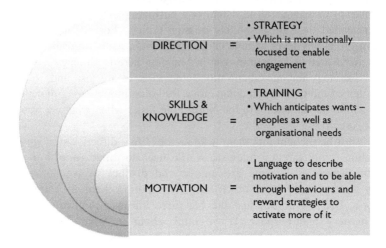

DIRECTION	=	• STRATEGY • Which is motivationally focused to enable engagement
SKILLS & KNOWLEDGE	=	• TRAINING • Which anticipates wants – peoples as well as organisational needs
MOTIVATION	=	• Language to describe motivation and to be able through behaviours and reward strategies to activate more of it

Figure 1.5 Business evolution

If we now rate ourselves on a 10-point scale for (S) and (M), we get a percentage number as to how well we are performing (P).

Activity 1.4

In your current role, rate yourself out of 10 for how skilful and knowledgeable you are. When you have done this rate yourself again out of 10 for how motivated you are. Do not simply think about this rating as being this moment or just today: reflect on how skilful/motivated you've been over the last six months. Then multiply the two numbers together: you have your own self-assessment.

If your score is above 80%, you are in the zone of performance; if you are 61–80%, then you are performing at a high level, but could go even higher; if you score 36–60%, then most likely you are not satisfied with your own performance and know you can do better; and if you score 35% or below, then something is fundamentally causing you problems in both your skills and your motivation.

Having done this, you also might like to now ask someone you know, like and trust to give you their feedback on the P = S × M exercise. Does their evaluation or perception of you match your own? It is very easy to either be hard on yourself, or alternatively to delude yourself about your performance levels. What is important is to understand yourself better and to take steps to improve performance: is it skills or is it motivation that is causing you to perform poorly? If you think about it, to be in the 80+% zone requires that your skills *and* motivation are at least 9/10 each. This, then, is a serious challenge.

Finally, we ask you, if you manage or lead a team, to think about your people in this way. Why not consider their performance in terms of $P = S \times M$, and then compare the results with any standard metrics that you currently use?[17] Is there a correlation?

But we can go further than this, for the formula as it stands only measures or defines the elements of actual performance. What about *probability* of performance success? And this is where our friend from earlier comes in: the attitude of commitment. This is, perhaps, that extra bit that firmly links motivation to engagement, for we have the energy and then the will too.

What, then, drives commitment? How is commitment established or built up in our will? One simple but explanatory theory[18] is that our commitment to anything has two vital components: one, we become committed when we perceive the value of a goal. We see why we are doing it and why it is important to us; in short, as we mentioned before regarding purpose, the goal becomes imbued with meaning for us. But that is not a sufficient reason in itself to activate real commitment. For, secondly, we must believe that there is a likelihood that we can achieve the goal, that we can be successful in pursuing it. If the goal seems impossible to achieve, then we are highly unlikely to commit to it. So this is a delicate balancing act: we need worthwhile goals and at the same time a strong probability that we can achieve them. Note, that a goal that we could achieve without any effort at all hardly merits the name of a goal, or of being worthwhile; the goal needs to stretch us, yet be attainable.

With these two factors in mind the performance formula can be expanded (Figure 1.6) to include commitment – keeping in mind that we are now talking about its probability or likelihood of being realised – which is an important aspect of employee engagement.

But as Commitment = Value of Goal + Likelihood of Success, then this now gives:

This is our PROBABILITY of performance success

Figure 1.6 Performance formula number two – probability of success

We need to be clear here that both performance formulas one and two are simply models; we have found them to be accurate and to work in most situations, but there will always be exceptions. However, as with all good models and maps, they help us focus on the real issues that bedevil our abilities to get results. Now, with performance formula two, we can think about not just skills and motivation, but also whether our employees are committed (Figure 1.7), and what commitment means. Do employees find the organisational mission, vision, values and goals important? Are they meaningful to them? And, given the goals that they are directed to achieve, how likely do they feel they can achieve them?

Activity 1.5

If you have done Activity 1.4, then let's re-consider this data, only this time bringing in the commitment variables. Skills and motivation are now to be scored out of 5:

My current skill (S) level out of 5 is:
My current motivation (M) level out of 5 is:
Add these two numbers together (S + M) = a score out of 10.

Consider now the biggest or most important or consequential work-related goal that you are trying to achieve? Write it down.

My biggest work goal is:
Score yourself out of 5 for how valuable that goal is to you. Then do the same for how likely it is that you perceive you can achieve that goal.

The value of this goal (V) to me out of 5 is:
The likelihood (L) of my achieving this goal out of 5 is:

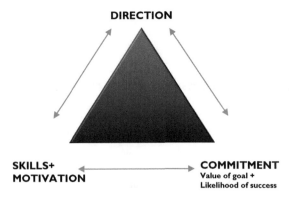

Figure 1.7 Performance triangle number two – commitment

Add these two numbers together (V + L) = a score out of 10.
Finally, to get your probability of performance success multiply your two numbers, $(S + M) \times (V + L)$, to get your % score.

Having done this, you will be in a much better position to begin to understand what this means for any employees you are managing. These variables are critical for you to understand and utilise if you are going to overcome barriers and get employee engagement. Keep in mind, as we said before, that this model is an approximation (albeit a good and powerful one); but also keep in mind that perfection is the enemy of progress. To understand this – without making it a fetish[19] – is a huge step forward in understanding engagement.

And so we come to a fifth barrier to engagement: the practicalities of how we measure it! For when we think about a business or an organisation we know that we are pretty – and rightly so – obsessed with measuring how we are doing. Any organisation really has four major functions (Figure 1.8) that drive its activities.

It should be clear just from looking at this that finance, marketing and sales, and operations are all well measured! Indeed, people – and leaders – often tend to judge their organisation based simply on one of two quite limited metrics: for example, sales volume (turnover) and profitability. But it should be equally obvious that the problem comes in the people quadrant where the data is no longer quantitative, or where there are typically no metrics, and where the qualitative data, such as it is, is often considered disputatious and 'soft'. A good

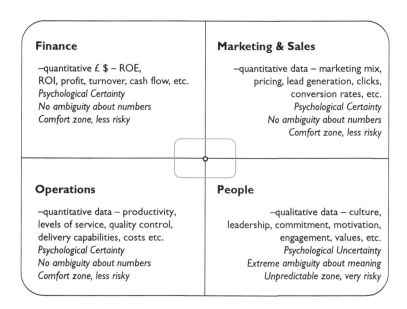

Figure 1.8 Four major functions of organisations

example might be performance appraisal results, which often seem irrelevant or at variance compared with, say, customer satisfaction or sales figures.[20]

The other aspect to notice, of course, is the fact that where we have metrics – in the first three quadrants – we tend to have a sense of certainty; a sense of certainty means we reduce risk because we avoid ambiguity.[21] That is why so many leaders never stray beyond their comfort zone, for who wants to embrace ambiguity and all the uncertainty that that entails? To do so, we think, is to be a real hero or heroine; and to do so is a necessary requirement of where we are now in organisational development and its need for employee engagement.

But Mapping Motivation here comes to the assistance of those who, if they are prepared to leave their comfort zones a little, can at least get some metrics about this people ambiguity. Motivational Maps describe, measure, monitor and ultimately maximise motivation. As we have already said, probably some 70% of engagement is down to motivation. So let's now consider this aspect of engagement through the motivational lens.

First, if we consider our number one performance matrix to be skills × motivation, we find four well-established possibilities for employees (Figure 1.9).

The job of management is to move as many employees as possible into the high motivation/high skill quadrant. This is not an easy task, considering that it

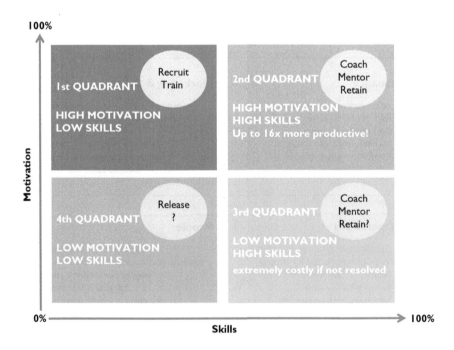

Figure 1.9 Four quadrants of performance

takes, in our experience, approximately a year to eighteen months to move from one quadrant to the next.

Activity 1.6

If you are a manager, take your list of team members: now allocate them to each of the four quadrants. Ask yourself, what percentage do you have of highly motivated and highly skilled people in your team, and what percentage is in each of the other three quadrants? Is there a 'skew' in percentage numbers in any one or two quadrants? What might that mean?

In the first quadrant there is a learning process necessarily going on, as skill levels are low; sometimes slow, but meticulous, and sometimes fast, but pressurised, yet with a high level of enthusiasm, as usually we are dealing with new recruits or teams. Individuals and teams in this quadrant are very much in the present, getting to grips with what needs to be learned. In the second quadrant we are looking at efficiency in the range of 80%+ and this needs to be maintained through assessing the changing motivational needs. Individuals and teams here will probably have a future-orientation as well as a positive, high success culture. In the third quadrant, conversation is either present- or past-orientated, clock watching is commonplace, and there is low level involvement – skills yes; motivation and engagement, no. This third quadrant is almost certainly the most difficult to deal with: often the employees who are de-motivated and disengaged – but highly skilled – are those who have been in the organisation a long time. They have become cynical, negative and adept at playing the system; what to do with them? The fourth quadrant is invariably for those who are a complete misfit with the organisation and its culture. Even when they are new recruits (and that incidentally means there is something seriously awry with the organisation's recruitment procedures and processes for them to be employed in the first instance) they will tend to have a past-orientation. Why? Because there is no future for them where they are, and usually no present either since they won't want to commit to the learning and the energy they need now, so they focus on the better times they had before. Thus, they are on a downward spiral and often want to take others down with them: it is a lonely state and so they want to share their misery. Beware, too, of blame – it's not *their* fault they are failing – so they will tend to foul-mouth the organisation.

But the point to make now should be obvious: having employees in quadrants one, three and four is costing employers – organisations – money, time and other significant factors too. To put this in perspective, in the UK in 2016, 137.3 million days[22] were lost through absence (sickness), costing – a median figure – some £11 billion! This is an extraordinarily high amount. This equates to 8.1 days lost per year in the public sector, and 5.1 days in the private sector.[23] While this figure is falling from a much higher number in the 1990s, this may not necessarily be for a good reason.[24]

But more generally, what is it costing? What do low levels of motivation and engagement really mean for an organisation?

Activity 1.7

If you are a manager or executive responsible for a team, or teams, even a whole organisation, or perhaps an outsider viewing an organisation you know something about, how much would you estimate low motivation is costing the organisation? Furthermore, make a list of all the areas in which you think low motivation is making a significant impact.

This (Figure 1.10) is a devastating indictment of what happens when employee motivation and engagement is not a priority. It is, perhaps, the last

What happens	Its Consequences
Employee Turnover – Up – employees leave	Costs £4.13bn per year UK across 5 sectors, £30K Per Person
Productivity – Down	Employees can be 16 Times Less Productive according to Pareto Principle
Absence Rates – Up – 'sickies'	Generates Low Morale, Low Energy, Low Self-Esteem
Recruitment Costs – Up – to replace lost & absent employees	Spent on Ads, Online Media, on Recruitment Agencies, and the Selection process itself
Fire-fighting – Up – as qualified and competent employees leave	Causes Stress and Health issues – so further absenteeism
Customers – Down – losing customers	Because Service is Poor, because employees they had a relationship with have gone
Reputation – Down – poor service and servicing the customer	This creates negative PR – typically one unhappy customer tells 13 others about their experience
Training Costs – Up to remedy the employee issues	But is the Training relevant? Tends to be Skills driven but motivation Is the issue – more waste of money?
Outsourcing Costs – Up – in order to compensate for insufficient employees, numerically and qualitatively	This becomes a Consultants' Paradise! Lots of fees paid to them!!!
Failure – Net Asset Value of the Organization goes Down	So Blame and Despair go Up – and we are in more danger of complete collapse

Figure 1.10 Low motivation within an organisation: 10 key symptoms

symptom that is the most telling of all, and is the result of the preceding nine: the net asset value of the organisation depreciates; this is very serious. Earlier, we talked about one of the barriers to engagement being 'capacity' – the lack of time that organisations felt they had in which to accomplish such an ambitious programme as employee engagement. This concept of capacity – what we are capable of – is also a useful idea when we consider employee productivity.

Activity 1.8

Study Figure 1.11. Consider, first, your own work and how you use time in accomplishing tasks relevant to your role. Nobody can work flat-out 100% of the time; so, how much time is spent relaxing? Then, consider how much time may be deliberately wasted – appearing to work, perhaps, but actually, for example, engaging in personal calls, social media chit-chat or games. But, too, what about 'unconsciously' being unproductive: the sort of work whereby one moves paper clips about and persuades one's self that one is working – 'tidying' the desk or sorting folders and so on – but not getting anywhere with important goals. And finally, there is real work: what percentage of time is spent doing that?

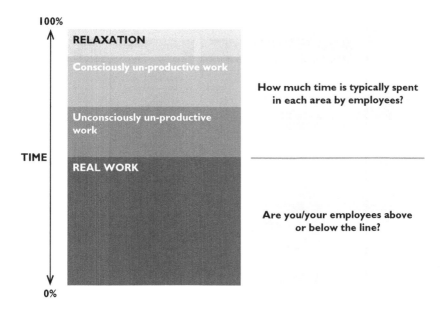

Figure 1.11 Productivity of demotivated employees

Having done that, consider a demotivated employee within your organisation and how they use their time? What is your calculation of their time spent not doing 'real work'? How does that translate when you scale it up to review a whole team of employees?

From our observations, working with hundreds of organisations, we think that the typical profile of productivity for the demotivated versus the motivated employee (given that there is, as Mapping Motivation shows, a wide spectrum) goes something like that shown in Figure 1.11 (and in presenting this to hundreds of CEOs and other managing directors we have found very little disagreement with our figures). This, then, means that the motivated member of staff (Figure 1.12) will use some 35% more of their time on 'real work' – and keep in mind that when they are working their performance levels can be anything from 4 to 16 times higher. Thus, we have a situation in which the highly motivated, highly engaged employee spends more actual time on the job (Figure 1.12), as well as almost certainly doing it better and to a higher quality. This, clearly, is a compounding interest effect.

What does this all mean as we reflect on the barriers to achieving employee engagement? One can take any number of studies, but we like one that really clearly and decisively demonstrated the full and motivational benefits of striving for employee engagement; that engagement and motivation led to the results shown in Figure 1.13.

Simply put, motivated employees will:

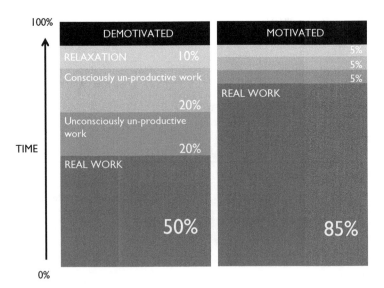

Figure 1.12 Productivity of demotivated employee versus motivated employee

Figure 1.13 Key motivational benefits of engagement
Source: Improving staff engagement: a practical toolkit, NHS Employers & O.C. Tanner, Issue 68: Nov 2009.

- work harder – INPUT more
- look for new ways to 'add value' – PROCESS better
- find direct ways to innovate – OUTPUT increase
- unleash the organisation's potential for – GROWTH.

With all these benefits in mind, then it becomes almost absurd to say 'we don't need engagement' and to be taken seriously as an organisation or business in the twenty-first century. Furthermore, the benefits clearly establish the strategic and imperative nature of the engagement programme. We established that there were five major barriers to implementing engagement: lack of senior commitment, lack of time and resources, rampant ego, inertia or status quo, and the question of how to measure motivation and engagement. This chapter has gone some considerable way to addressing the issue of a lack senior commitment by addressing the bottom line of what's in it for the organisation. As we unpack our seven-step process in the following chapters we are going to offer insights into how these other barriers can also be broken down.

Notes

1 J.A.C. Brown, *The Social Psychology of Industry*, Penguin (1958):

> There can be little doubt that the major problem in industry today is the problem of suitable leadership. There are far too many petty Hitlers in factories who are not only working off their own mental conflicts on others to the detriment of the psychological health of the community but are psychologically incapable of delegating authority and making industry more democratic.

2 David Bowles and Cary Cooper, *The High Engagement Work Culture*, Palgrave Macmillan (2012): they refer to ego as acting 'like a psychological virus' and in particular they establish through extensive evidence and research that ego-driven executives are pre-eminently concerned about obtaining excessive remuneration without corresponding performance. This palpably demotivates and disengages employees.
3 Wittily, Harold Geneen, the legendary boss of ITT, once commented: 'The worst disease which can afflict business executives in their work is not, as popularly supposed, alcoholism; it's egotism.' Cited on Self Help Community website: http://bit.ly/2hkbEoc.
4 David Guest, Professor of Organisational Psychology and Human Resource Management at Kings College London, was cited in the MacLeod Report as making this observation.
5 The MacLeod Report, David MacLeod et al., *Engaging for Success: Enhancing Performance through Employee Engagement*, Office of Public Sector Information (2009).
6 Philip Crosby, *Let's Talk Quality*, Penguin (1992).
7 One of the reasons we believe psychometrics have been so prevalent in organisational work over the last 40 or so years is because they tend to be behavioural in nature, which means management like to use them to control staff. Clearly, as soon as employees become aware that they are being 'controlled', then engagement is out of the window.
8 Tom O'Byrne, CEO Great Place to Work, argues that 'the focus shouldn't be performance'. *Employee Engagement*, Media Planet (September 2016).
9 For more on this, see James Sale, *Mapping Motivation*, Routledge (2016).
10 This issue is covered in considerable detail in James Sale earlier book, *Mapping Motivation* (2016), and with Bevis Moynan, *Mapping Motivation for Coaching*, Routledge (2018). This account, whilst containing some overlap in information, also provides new and more advanced ideas.
11 'Skills' is the generic term which we use to incorporate also knowledge, or what is sometimes called competence.
12 This of course, as a matter of principle, goes beyond meaning in organisations and businesses: all religions suggest or insist their adherents choose the 'right' path because not to do so has usually dire consequences both in this life and – where one believes – the next as well.
13 Daniel Pink, *Drive: The Surprising Truth about What Motivates Us*, Canongate (2010). We like this book a lot, but don't wholly agree with all his conclusions. For us, for example, Mastery is not a primary motivator but a subset of an even more primary one: Creativity which, to be fully accomplished, requires Mastery.

14 Man's search for meaning – the title of a book by Victor Frankl – is essentially part of what might be termed his/her 'spiritual' nature. This must not be confused with religion, but religion is one possible outcome of that primary search. Clearly, it is the highest part of being human; and mind, emotion and body, ideally, generate their alignment from perceived meaning.

15 In *Mapping Motivation for Coaching*, see above, we talk about 'dreams' as ultimately a source of all our desires, imagination and expectations, and so beliefs; and we say, 'What is strange is that from such unprepossessing, insubstantial, evanescent materials the reality of our lives is built.'

16 This formula is explored and explained in a lot more detail in *Mapping Motivation*, and *Mapping Motivation for Coaching*, see above.

17 Metrics could literally be almost anything: appraisal ratings, sales figures, calls per day, customer satisfaction ratings, quality and defects, and so on, depending on sector and role.

18 E. Tory Higgins, *Beyond Pleasure and Pain: How Motivation Works*, Oxford University Press (2014).

19 A fetish here meaning either a slavish interpretation of the numbers; and a good thing always to do with this type of process is to invite someone you trust to give you a view (where they are in a position to do so) of your 'accounting'. For example, is there perception of your commitment numbers (V and L) the same as theirs? Or, the obsession of so many to try to turn managing and motivating people into an exact science whereby everything is researched to the nth degree and nothing can be done until we have every single number and every number must stack up; in other words, we cannot act till research tells us we have total certainty! Truly, an absurd position to be in when dealing with the psychological ambiguities of people. Of course, the importance of research generally we are not disputing, and this book itself is a contribution based on our research and experience.

20 Hence in the last ten years the increasing frustration and abandonment of performance appraisals by many leading companies worldwide. Our book, *Mapping Motivation for Appraisals*, from Routledge, will soon be available to show how performance appraisals can be used far more effectively than they currently are.

21 It was Cardinal de Retz who said, 'One abandons ambiguity at one's peril'. By staying in the comfort zones, paradoxically, we increase our risk, for effectively we are not addressing the biggest single issue for our organisation: retaining, motivating and engaging our key people.

22 According to the Office for National Statistics, http://bit.ly/2moHN1q.

23 Taking median figures extrapolated by Personnel Today, http://bit.ly/1MTQmUW. Ideally, we think these figures could become lower still – if motivation, engagement and well-being were truly operative.

24 'Sir Cary Cooper, professor of organisational psychology and health at the Manchester Business School at Manchester University, said that people were frightened of taking time off for sickness, and that presenteeism was a big threat to UK workplace productivity'. http://bbc.in/2yoguaR.

Chapter 2

Understanding the MacLeod Report, four engagement enablers and Motivational Mapping

In Chapter 1 we looked at some of the barriers to employee engagement and at the same time pointed out that engagement or the lack thereof has a serious impact on all businesses and organisations. Also, we mentioned that there are many models attempting to explain what employee engagement actually is, but on top of that complexity it is also vital not to try to take a model off the shelf and mechanically apply it your organisation. The reason for this caution should be obvious: one size does not fit all, and one key aspect of any engagement programme we seek to implement is that it must emotionally connect with our people; for if it doesn't, then we will fail. But to connect emotionally means that employees themselves must perceive the programme as authentic and relevant. Perhaps the most dreaded phrase in all management practice – guaranteed to kill stone-dead any initiative in any organisation – is this one: 'a tick-box exercise'. And tick-box exercises are precisely the result of the mechanical application of ideas and processes – sometimes very good ones, such as performance appraisal – which staff come to hate,[1] resent, and to regard as a pointless waste of time. Thus, good ideas are destroyed simply because no-one has really bothered to understand them properly and assess their true fitness-for-purpose in the context and culture of the host organisation.

With this in mind, then, we need to be aware of the bad news; that is, bad news for people who do not like to think. Maybe they prefer to follow orders, or to have automated systems, or to take the easy route; but whatever their reason, they avoid thinking through what they really need to do to make engagement work. But thinking this through is what we have to do for *our* context and *our* particular culture; in other words, for *our* people.

In 2009 the UK government produced a report, which came to be known as the MacLeod Report,[2] which sought to consolidate best practice in the UK on enabling employee engagement. In doing this it indicated clearly that engagement was a national priority if Britain intended to remain prosperous and competitive in the global economy. According to MacLeod there are four major enablers of employee engagement (Figure 2.1), but these enablers, it must be said, require an alternative mind-set to that of normal business and organisational practice; this

Figure 2.1 Four enablers of employee engagement

alternative mind-set is about our perception of how we see our people: as a cost and a problem? Or, as an asset and a solution?

What do these four enablers mean?

Activity 2.1

Consider the four headings, which are based on the enablers put forward in the MacLeod Report. What do they mean to you? What do they suggest needs to happen within an organisation? Why aren't these enablers happening now in an organisation you work in or know well? And which of these four enablers do you think – if you could choose only one – is the most important?

1. Visible, empowering leadership
2. Engaging managers
3. Employee voice
4. Organisational integrity

Visible, empowering leadership sounds self-evidently vital[3] to the welfare not only of the employees and to their engagement, but to the prosperity of the organisation itself, especially long term. But specifically here what fuels engagement is leadership providing a strong, strategic narrative about the organisation. What this means is: staff can understand where the organisation has come from and where it's going, and in that way they can see where they fit into its trajectory. This needs considerably more explanation.

Professor Brian Cox[4] once observed that 'narrative may be regarded as a primary act of mind'. What this means is that human beings understand and makes sense of their lives through stories. Children are excited by and love stories, and we as adults are no different; we all have a tale to tell, and these tales – these stories – especially when we tell them to ourselves, form our identity. Indeed, our self-concept and beliefs about ourselves emerge much more powerfully, albeit sometimes obliquely, through our stories than through our rational and 'thought through' philosophies; often the latter are simply pegs or markers we flag up to impress others.

The point about stories is that they grab our imagination;[5] or, more accurately, the point about *good* stories is they stir our imaginations. Bad, tedious or clichéd stories bore and repel us. But the thing is, once the imagination is excited, then our emotions also come into play, which means our vital energies are aroused. We develop motivation, power and focus.

Clearly, this is very relevant to employee engagement in at least two major ways. First, each organisation has its own narrative about it origins, purpose and future, but so does each employee. How do their respective narratives match or mesh? This 'matching' is effectively a resonance – an affinity; we will want to work for an organisation where we 'feel' their narrative extends and continues our own story; that as we contribute to their narrative, our own is being enriched. Second, on what basis would we decide that there was a match between our story and that of the organisation? For many it will be a rational activity; at a basic level this might mean, 'the organisation pays me the wage I want'. At a more complex, but still rational, level, this might mean, 'I agree with this organisation's stance on animal testing'. But the truth is, just as when purchasing, people do not often act logically (they buy on emotional grounds and seek the reasons afterwards to justify the purchase), so in 'buying' a job at a specific organisation we 'feel' there is a fit. In short, we feel motivated by some organisations and not by others, and usually we are not consciously aware of why this is.

Thus, we come to the point where motivation is relevant to the concept of a visible, empowering leadership because, amongst other reasons, it is part of the strategic narrative. The effective narrative has to be energising, and thereby emotional, and this means that narrative too has motivational qualities or elements that will correlate with Motivational Mapping. In fact, if we take the three primary groupings of the motivators – RAG – we could ask whether the story is primarily about Relationships or Achievements or Growth.

And if we ask that question, then we are faced with another fascinating aspect of motivation: namely, its correlation with tenses, or time. Put another way, what is a key characteristic of relationship-type motivators? Relationships for all of us strengthen the further into the past they stretch; normally, our strongest relationships are our earliest, which is why we can only with great difficulty shake off our family ties.[6] Similarly, if we are achievement-orientated in our motivators, then we tend to be present-tense orientated, because achievement requires us doing things in the *now*! Obviously, too, growth motivators predicate a future orientation, since growing implies a state in the future that we will become.

With this in mind, then, we could ask: does the story have a past orientation, as when an organisation focusses, for example, on the fact that it was established in, say, 1950 or 1850 or even 1750 and has a long history and tradition;[7] or a present orientation, in which products and services are very much geared around today's needs and what is contemporary; or, is there a future orientation in which the visionary qualities of the organisation hope to anticipate developments of tomorrow and beyond. In addition, of course, there will be organisations, as there are people, with mixed mixed motivational profiles and tense-related orientations.[8] These need to be dealt with on a case by case basis.

Activity 2.2

What do you think are the characteristics of an organisation which is:

*   Relationship/past orientated?
*   Achievement/present orientated?
*   Growth/future orientated?

Jot down your ideas. Given your own Motivational Maps' profile, which type appeals to you the most? Or, put another way, what sort of organisation (or self-employment) would you prefer to work in? Why?

Here are some key ideas based on Mapping Motivation that characterise organisational life and what is important to an organisation.

It is worth saying at this point that there is no better or worse RAG type any more than there are better or worse motivators: context is everything. In one sense we need to focus on our strengths., for example, if we are 'red' then we 'get results'. In another sense, paradoxically, we need to be very aware of where we have 'Achilles' heels' that may trip us up. For example, if we are 'red', we need to remember that we do not pay enough attention to the motivations of our employees (green) or even that we do not think long term (blue). The RAG types, metaphorically, are linked to the colours green, red and blue because in one important sense these three primary colours combined make pure and whole light – a difficult balance to achieve.

Seeing how employees' motivators, then, drive their narratives and so provide a fit, or mismatch, between themselves and the organisation is highly significant. A central concept here is self-awareness on behalf on the employees, on the one hand, and the organisation on the other. We can achieve our greatest successes where there is alignment, and it is also possible – though more difficult and more unlikely – to achieve organisational success where there is not motivational alignment, but the organisation and the individual consciously and deliberately embrace each other's differing perspectives on the basis of solving a problem that could not otherwise be solved by either without the other. This is effectively, and usually, going to be where the employee has a 'talent' (which is a combination of naturally strong interests, motivations and skill sets) that compensates for some deficiency, or Achilles' heel, within the organisation. This scenario can be found in any type of organisation,[9] but often it is to be found in what Charles Handy[10] called 'existential' or Dionysian or 'person' cultures. This inevitably creates 'mavericks' and these can be very successful, but the danger can be that no matter whether they fit or not, the maverick (perceived as a 'rain-maker') is excused in all or any of their (potentially) obnoxious behaviours – indeed is insulated[11] from their consequences – because they are perceived to be too valuable to the organisation to be lost.[12]

Given this and these dangers, then, how might we review employee and organisational Motivational Mapping?

Activity 2.3

Take a close look at Figure 2.3 where we have extracted some core information from Figure 2.2. We come down here to seven key areas where we have preferences. This exercise can be done personally – from your perspective thinking about an organisation (which can include the choice of 'your' own organisation or self-employment or your own business, and imagining what it will be like) that you work for or wish to join. Or it can be done from an organisational point of view, considering the kind of people that we wish to recruit, or those we have in situ and how they fit or not with our motivational strategic narrative. Keep positively in mind that there is always the choice of 'mixed'[13] (M) if you find the first three choices too constraining; many motivational profiles will be mixed. In column three we invite you to compare your answers in columns two and four: is there a match or a mismatch? Try probing the implications of these answers. What, for example, is essential and what secondary for you? What needs more clarity and focus? And, how might one feel if one were working in an organisation where some six or all seven of the choices were aligned with the organisation?

Activity 2.4

From the organisational point of view, it is now important to consider, or reconsider, one's strategic narrative in terms of its motivational component, for in doing so we increase its attractiveness to all stakeholders, especially employees. To do this, set your current narrative against the seven options in Figure 2.3 and ask which ones are you 'touching'? If one does this in advance of actually completing an organisational Motivational Map, one would still have a strong idea of which motivators are driving the organisation.[14]

Earlier, however, we asked which of the four employee enablers was the most important. The answer is probably the second one: engaging managers.[15] To be clear, engaging managers does not mean managers who are attractive to talk to, and have nice manners, as desirable as being 'engaging' in that sense might be. No, we are now at the heart of the matter: engaging managers are managers who have the ability – the skills – to engage their employees, and of course this means the ability to motivate them. Indeed, to be an 'engaging manager' is to be a 'motivating manager', and it stands to reason why this is the pivotal

	Perspective of	Mindset	People want	Process preferred	Persuaded by	Attracted to
Relationship						
(R)	PAST	This is how we do things here!	Loyalty/collaboration	Efficiency/systems	Proof	When in Rome …
Green	Continuity/quality	Why would we not do it like this?	Emotion	Slow decision-making	Relationships	Tribes/movements
	Values/commitment	Process-driven/rational	Stories	Change/risk aversion	Deference	Safety
Achievement	PRESENT	How do we achieve this?	Competitiveness	Effectiveness/goals	Results	Just do it …
(A)	Building/utility	What needs to happen now?	Things	Steady decision-making	Advantages	Control
Red	Hard Facts/soft facts	Outputs-led/experiential	Results-orientation	Change/risk calculated	Bottom line	Success
Growth	FUTURE	Where will we be in 5 years' time?	Initiative/experimentation	Holistic/idealistic big picture	Importance	Making a difference …
(G)	Envisioning/supremacy	How do we get to this point?	Ideas	Fast decision-making	First-mover	Autonomy
Blue	Creating/ideals	Ingenuity-focused/imaginative	Significance	Change/risk friendliness	Big picture	Uniqueness
Mixed RAG	Mixed	Mixed	Mixed	Mixed	Mixed	Mixed

Figure 2.2 Implications of RAG for organisational culture

	COLUMN 2		COLUMN 4
	Personal Career Narrative might be ...	Compare columns 2 and 4	Organisational Narrative suggests they are ...
Predominantly R or A or G or Mixed (M)?			
About Values or Facts or Ideals or (M)?			
Into Processes or Outputs or Ingenuity or (M)?			
Likes Loyalty or Competitiveness or Experimentation or (M)?			
Works Efficiently or Effectively or Holistically or (M)?			
Influenced by Proof or Results or Importance or (M)?			
Prefers Safety or Success or Uniqueness or (M)?			

Figure 2.3 Reviewing motivational alignment

enabler: for it is the managers who directly impact the employee. Of course the other three enablers are vital too; it's a whole package, but empowering leaders and strategic narratives at the top are a step removed from the day-to-day activities of the employees. Similarly, the employees having a voice can only occur if the managers are engaging, whatever structure is in place. And finally, organisational integrity, whilst critical in the long term,[16] can be offset in the short and medium terms by your own personal and engaging manager. For it has truly been said that one does not leave a job, one always leaves a boss; and this will mostly be a non-engaging manager!

With this in mind, then, how do managers become 'engaging'? This is primarily about creating an environment in which motivation can thrive; motivational environments, in other words. To create such an environment is no easy thing, for if it were we would see a lot more of it; and also it is important to note that it is no easy option[17] to choose to do such a thing. Naturally, it should be obvious that it has to start at the top and work its way down. But that said, as a starter, here are three critical components (Figure 2.4) that the engaging manager must embrace.

Let's review these three essential components in a little more detail. First, what does it mean to have 'greater' motivation than the employees in the team, and why is this significant? It is certainly true that one could – and that people do – know intuitively whether one is, or one's boss is, more motivated than others in a team. After all, since motivation is energy it will manifest in all sorts of ways, behaviours and activities, and also in that more indefinable sense of enthusiasm for the work. That 'indefinable' sense is often contagious, and its absence is a form of lifelessness. But we can know much more accurately using Motivational Maps, and what we mean here is very specific. It would be best if the leader were the most motivated person on the team, but possibly unrealistic:

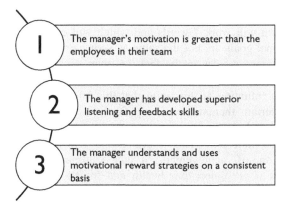

Figure 2.4 Three critical components of being an engaging manager

a new person joining freshly, for example, or a team member who is simply a tremendous and consistent resource, may well have the honour of being the 'most' motivated person in the team. So what we mean here is that if we do a Motivational Team Map based on all the team members, there will be an average motivational score for the team, and the engaging manager must have a score above that average. Furthermore, it ideally needs to be in the zone quadrant – or 81% and above – to be fully effective.

Why is this? First, and primarily, because the manager is the leader, the model for everybody else. This is the person we look to for a 'lead' on how things are supposed to be; not only that, but given that they are in a position of authority, we consciously or subconsciously assume that behaving like that is how we progress and get promoted. Thus, we take our cue from the manager. If, then, their motivation is less than ours, what does that tell us? Ultimately, it tells us we need not bother too much. And there is a further point here too: people tend to *resonate* at the frequency of those around them. High motivation is high energy is high frequency; low motivation is low energy is low frequency. We see this everywhere, in social as well as work situations. High-energy people bring out high energy in others, whereas low-energy people smother it, especially when they occupy dominant roles.

The engaging manager must, therefore, be a highly motivated manager. This is not a 'point-taken, duly-noted, box-ticked' kind of requirement. It means that the engaging manager actively seeks to be self-motivated, actively maintains high levels of motivation, and becomes through this a beacon of energy for others. Thus, it becomes a 'duty' almost (and that does seem a laborious word in the context of motivation) for every engaging manager to have a Motivational Action Plan (or MAP), and so it will come as no surprise to learn that every Motivational Map has, on page 14, a MAP to complete. It looks something like the one shown in Figure 2.5.

Activity 2.5

Review your Motivational Map. Use the information in your Map, especially regarding your top three motivators, to start creating motivational goals for yourself that you will work towards and which will energise you. Remember, these motivational goals are not the same as your work or organisational goals, but their importance resides in the fact that they *enable* you to achieve these work-related targets.

It is worth mentioning at this point that this book is going to return again and again to certain thematic preoccupations, and in doing so will provide more tools and techniques to sometimes do exactly the same thing: namely, to become more motivated. This is because, like health and fitness, motivation is not a one-off achievement; it is a continual process. We have to understand that if we ignore our health and fitness for any length of time, then we become unhealthy and unfit; so it is with motivation. The engaging manager consistently seeks to top-up his motivation batteries; sometimes this will involve well-established and familiar habits, but sometimes too there will

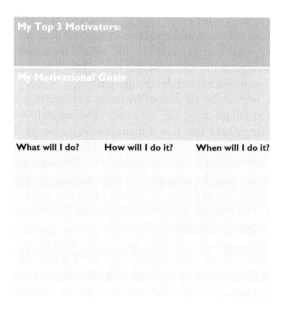

Figure 2.5 Your Motivational Action Plan (MAP)

be new ideas to help the engaging manager get just that bit more juice to boost them.

Our second critical component for being an engaging manager is to have developed superior listening and feedback skills. This point is, arguably, one of the most frustrating topics in the world! It is frustrating because management and management literature have been talking about these things for a long, long time, and yet in some respects little progress has been made. We talked earlier about the ego, about 'petty Hitlers', about top-down management styles that demotivate, disengage, and seriously depress employees across the world. Keep in mind, also, that the figure for engaged staff worldwide, which is approximately 30%, has remained static for years[18] despite all the investments in engagement and such-like programmes. What is to be said and what is to be done about this scenario?

First, in our view it is important to realise that the 80/20 rule, or Pareto principle, operates virtually all the time. Despite the continuing newspaper headlines of yet another management failure in yet another major corporation, there are pockets of excellence everywhere, and it is on their examples that we must build. Second, one reason why organisations rarely fully implement the development of listening and feedback skills at a superior level is because it has in the past – as with other 'soft' issues – never been taken too seriously; put another way, it has only ever been at best operationally convenient rather than strategically necessary. The MacLeod Report, along with lots of other research, now decisively confutes this position:

engagement is the strategic issue for long-term success. Finally, we have to keep reminding ourselves of what Brian Tracy[19] observed and which reinforces the necessity of making soft skills an imperative throughout an organisation: 'The way you treat people, what you say and do that affects them emotionally, is more important in bringing out the best in people than all the education, intelligence, or experience that you might have at doing your job.'

In brief, then, what is the essence of listening and feedback skills? First, they have to be practised till they are automatic and natural; the test of this is whether or not employees feel that a management technique is being used on them. As with a great actor, there should seem to be no technique, only presence – authenticity. Second, let's keep in mind why listening and (motivational) feedback are the two most important skills from the engagement perspective. To listen, to really listen[20] to someone, is a form of loving them, and we all have a deep inner need to be listened to in this way. And as for feedback, it satisfies the primary human need to be appreciated.[21]

Superior listening skills usually have five components that enabling managers need to be constantly aware of and practising (see Figure 2.6).

Attentiveness means actually and actively listening, as opposed to merely waiting to speak your turn. One useful tip here is consistently to lean forward whether sitting or standing, for this creates the impression of listening – and whether you are or not, eventually mind follows body and you will be listening if you continue in this posture.

A further tip is to use **rapid repeat**. If you have a problem actually listening, then try to give yourself a two-minute burst of this technique. Longer can be very exhausting! Basically, when someone is speaking to you, repeat in your mind exactly what they say as a sort of verbal echo (with a half second delay). Try to capture their intonation, volume and style of speech. This technique prevents you from trying to anticipate replying to them prematurely, whilst simultaneously drilling down their message at a deep level.

Pause before replying for up to 2–3 seconds, because it improves the quality of information you receive (because you hear more, and the slight delay means

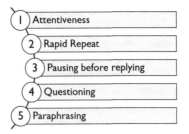

Figure 2.6 Five components of listening skills

you are less likely to react),[22] and it prevents upsetting the speaker by constantly interrupting and completing sentences for them. Pausing does not mean you cannot make supportive gestures, interjections and comments like, 'great'; it means you refrain from actually replying.

Questioning, and in particular asking open questions. These may be summarised as questions beginning HOW, WHAT and WHY, and probably fall in that order of importance. Initially, the single most powerful open question we can probably ask any employee is:

HOW can we improve
... your situation?
... your performance?
... our systems and processes?
... relationships within the team?
... our business?
... this organisation? Or,
... this ... whatever?

HOW potentially unlocks the magic of each individual's knowledge, skill and creativity. Just remember to be sparing of WHY questions as they can sometimes seem accusatory, as in 'why did you do that?' Obviously, tone of voice is crucial.

Paraphrase regularly. Paraphrasing[23] is a difficult and disappearing skill. It means to summarise to the speaker what you think they have said, but in your own words; also, it requires that you ask them for confirmation that you have understood them. 'Let me get this straight, what you're saying is ... Is that right?' Clearly, it is deeply gratifying for the speaker to say, 'Yes, that's right', but it is also gratifying for them to say, 'No, I didn't mean that. What I meant was ...' and so they the chance to clarify their ideas. The process is repeated until the speaker is sure the listener 'gets' what they are saying.

The combination of these five components used in a conversation with an employee is almost incalculably powerful. People, as Dale Carnegie noted some 70 or so years ago, desperately want to be listened to, and they will follow – adore! – the engaging manager who genuinely listens to them. But, of course, let's not forget that to listen takes time. We could be busy being important and issuing instructions, or we could be listening, really listening. What are we going to do?

Activity 2.6

How good are you at listening, really listening to your staff, or even to members of your own family, or your friends? Give yourself a score (see Figure 2.7) out of four where:

	4	3	2	I	0	TOTAL
Attentiveness						
Rapid Repeat						
Pause before replying						
Questioning – Open						
Paraphrasing						

Figure 2.7 Rating your listening skills

> *4 is outstanding*
> *3 is excellent*
> *2 is good*
> *1 is poor*
> *0 is not done at all*

for all five components of listening.

The possible maximum is 20 – multiply by 5 to get a % score. Aim to be at least 80+%. Identify the area(s) where you can improve your listening skills, and start practising.

If listening is the 'yin' of superior engaging manager skills, then the 'yang' is motivational feedback. We advocate active listening, but we can clearly see that as a 'skill', listening per se may appear somewhat passive. For this reason, perhaps, especially in macho-type cultures, because one who is listening does not seem to be *doing* much, its value is massively underrated. This of course is a huge mistake. But motivational feedback, on the other hand, is in its nature more overt, immediate and seemingly impactful. Everybody craves motivational feedback and the recognition and appreciation it properly bestows upon the recipient.

To grasp more fully the impact of motivational feedback we need to consider that the word 'feedback' is a somewhat dry, academic, and scientific word. If we look for a synonym for motivational feedback that expresses its true nature, then perhaps the best we can find is 'soul food'. Yes, soul food conveys just that sense of nourishment that the individual needs at a deep level. Thus, as an organisation we must become purveyors of soul food: engaging managers provide a continual diet of soul food to nourish their teams, and their teams love it and love them.

However, we need to be clear as to what motivational feedback actually is; for it is not simply 'praise'. We are all too familiar with the person who, after we have completed some task or job, says to us, 'Well done', or 'Good job', and like water off a duck's back it makes absolutely no impression at all; in fact, we often discount it.

Activity 2.7

If motivational feedback is not simply praise, then what is it? Jot down all the characteristics that you think constitute motivational feedback. Think back to situations when you perceived that you received it. What were its essential ingredients?

In carrying out the five steps in Figure 2.8, to maintain motivation keep being specific, simple and sincere at all times, and remember that point two is the single most important constituent of motivational feedback. It is when you say to the employee not just what their action or words were, which is mere photography, but explain its beneficial implications – which is art! – then they know you have truly noticed them. So, to give an example of this, suppose your employee has just dealt with a difficult customer on the telephone and you have heard the whole exchange between them. The dialogue might run something like this:

Manager:

1. INFORM – Sam, thanks for taking that call. Mr Smith is a really difficult customer and is always complaining about something or other ...
2. EXPLAIN CONSEQUENCE – You know you saved me probably half an hour with the way you handled that ...
3. PRAISE – you are really good at dealing with difficult customers; I am truly impressed ...

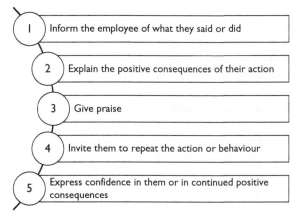

Figure 2.8 Five constituents of motivational feedback

4.   INVITE REPETITION – please keep this up; it's going to make all our lives so much easier ...
5.   EXPRESS CONFIDENCE – I have total confidence in you, Sam; I could leave the office and I know everything will be taken care of.

Soft skills are a vital element of being an engaging manager. But they are not sufficient in themselves to create full engagement from the workforce. Richard Brimble[24] correctly observed that, 'No amount of soft skills training will change the underlying culture'. Which leads us to our third essential component for the engaging manager: that they must understand and use motivational reward strategies on a consistent basis. This is something which is really double-layered. Yes, at the first layer the engaging manager must use these core ideas; but on the second layer, this is really a cultural, strategic and organisational issue. It is true that any given manager could use the ideas of motivational reward strategies without reference to the wider organisation, just as any dynamic individual can – despite the system – make a difference through their own endeavours. We must not forget Peter Drucker's wise observation that, 'Whenever anything is being accomplished, it is being done, I have learned, by a monomaniac with a mission'.[25] However, that said, we want to extend the franchise of motivational reward strategies much wider than simply the odd monomaniac here and there! So whilst we shall comment on this briefly here, it is necessary that we return to this issue in much greater detail later.

So what are we talking about? We are talking about the fact that one size does not fit all, that standardised rewards ultimately demotivate, and that if we want managers to be engaging, then they need to understand the motivational profile of each individual in the team, as well as the team itself, if they are going to target appropriate rewards. In the past we have – perhaps inappropriately, given that it's a military metaphor – referred to the difference between 'carpet-bombing' a target versus 'precision-missiling' it. The former hopes an appropriate target will be hit, but suffers the double disadvantages of massive collateral damage combined with wasted resources; whereas the latter solves the problem in one go, economically and effectively. And if we want to perhaps have a better metaphor – not a military one – then maybe we should think about parents at Christmas (or any major holiday period). There are those who don't really consider their children as individuals, but blanket them with presents that they may or may not want. Often, too, choosing items that perhaps the parents themselves would have liked as youngsters. The child is often distracted by the amount of presents they receive on the day, but that soon wears off as it becomes apparent to them over the days ahead that this is just 'more stuff'. Contrast that with the child, or children, who are truly seen as individuals, and whom the parents really know well: they may only get them one present, but it is the present they really wanted all along, and for this are truly happy, truly grateful.

In a sense, then, this is exactly what Motivational Maps is providing: the opportunity for each manager to give each member of staff what they really want. And the beauty of it is that this is not difficult and in real terms would actually cost no more than the laborious efforts that are currently made to 'reward' employees. What are these rewards? Well, costly perks – not targeted, financial incentives – invariably short-term, formal solutions for people development; tick-box orientated; indeed, anything in which command-and-control managers appear to be thinking about their staff, but are not. Again, as Richard Brimble[26] observed: 'It's just easier to run a course than to solve the real problems'.

In the succeeding chapters we will be developing the ideas in this chapter further, and also taking a detailed look at the other two enablers: employee voice and organisational integrity.

Notes

1 W. Edwards Deming, the great quality guru, said, 'Put a good person in a bad system and the bad system wins, no contest'. Attributed to February 1993 Deming Four Day seminar in Phoenix, Arizona.
2 The MacLeod Report, David MacLeod et al., *Engaging for Success: Enhancing Performance through Employee Engagement*, Office of Public Sector Information (2009).
3 'Senior leadership is regarded as the most critical driver of sustainability within a business and nearly half of businesses (44%) believe engagement with business leaders will be the most important factor in successfully implementing a sustainability strategy over the next three years.' Economist Intelligence Unit (EIU) & Coca-Cola Enterprises, 2013; and also, 'Deloitte found that companies viewed as having particularly strong leadership could enjoy a stock market valuation premium of more than 15 per cent. Those seen as having ineffective leadership suffered discounts of up to 20 per cent'. Research by *The Times* newspaper, handout 12/6/ 2012.
4 Professor Brian Cox, *The Cox Report*, HMSO (1989).
5 To understand fully – if that were possible – the power of the imagination in our lives we have to leave the literature of management and visit the poets! It was W.B. Yeats who said, 'I am now certain that the imagination has some way of lighting on the truth that reason has not, and its commandments, delivered when the body is still and the reason silent, are the most binding we can ever know' from *Ideas of Good and Evil* (1903).
6 Which of course we would only want to do if they were severely negative; even so, cutting ties with our family or a family member does not mean that they no longer continue to affect us, our behaviour and our thinking.
7 So, for example, of the past, Lloyds Bank's 2017 advertising campaign explicitly majors on 'By your side for 250 years'; of the present, a company like WPP Plc, an advertising company founded in 1985 and which serves its clients worldwide provides them with messages of 'contemporary' relevance; of the future, a company like Tesla, founded in 2003 and whose product line anticipates the demise of gas-fuelled cars. This is not to pigeon-hole these organisations in any way; Lloyds Bank likes to advertise its long tradition in order to suggest it will go on making a future impact. Every organisation eventually has to re-invent itself; but the point is the 'feel' and the 'energy' of these, and other organisations, always has a time tense attached to it, and these are linked to their motivators.

8 Often time also suggests certain 'values' that appeal to different people. So, classically, if an organisation has been around a long time it may well project the idea of 'quality'; an organisation that operates in the present may well project the idea of 'relevance' or 'practicality'; and a future-orientated organisation will suggest 'vision' or 'innovation'. But this is not to be prescriptive.

9 Charles Handy, *Gods of Management*, Pan Books (1978). Handy identified four primary types of culture: Club Culture (Zeus – one central leader pulling the strings e.g. strong CEOs often found in entrepreneurial ventures; Role Culture (Apollo – ordered and highly structured e.g. life insurance companies); Task Culture (Athene – focused on problem solving e.g. consultancies) and lastly, Existential Culture – Dionysian, often where extreme expertise is so highly valued, the individual is more important than the organisation e.g. film stars, ivy-league professors, ad agency 'names', etc.

10 Charles Handy, *Understanding Organisations*, Penguin (1993).

11 A recent example would be Harvey Weinstein in the film industry in the USA; in the UK it seems clear that Jimmy Saville, a notorious sexual predator, was protected for decades by the industry and the organisation he worked in.

12 And here we refer back to Chapter 1 for what this can create: ego-driven monsters!

13 For reasons of space we will necessarily need to be extremely brief in covering the Mixed (M) profile, and also, as we have already pointed out, M needs to be considered on a case by case basis. But as with the other three options of R, A and G there are always going to be positives and negatives. The negative aspects of M are likely to be a combination that produces uncertainty, tension and indecisiveness as the motivators – what we want – drive the organisation in opposite directions. Offset against that, the positives might be more balance, a fuller spectrum of options, and diversity. Again, as we always say, context is everything.

14 For more on this, see our forthcoming book in this Routledge series: *Mapping Motivation for Strategy*.

15 Mark C. Crowley put it this way: 'Engagement largely comes down to whether people have a manager who cares about them, grows them and appreciates them'. Employee Engagement Isn't Getting Better and Gallup Shares the Surprising Reasons Why, Linkedin post, 9/12/2015, http://bit.ly/2kLVwke.

16 Bob Garrett, *The Fish Rots from the Head*, Harper Collins (1997) observed: 'An unethical base can take you forward for some years … But in the end there is always a reckoning-up to the detriment of all stakeholders.'

17 'By now it should be obvious that the "emotional" side of policy is not a soft option' – Bob Garrett, *The Fish Rots from the Head*, op. cit.

18 And what this also means, according to Brian Tracy, citing research from Robert Half International, is that 'the average person works at about 50% of capacity'. Brian Tracy, *Full Engagement*, American Management Association (2011). Also, Mark C Crowley, op. cit., specifically says, 'growth in engagement has remained flat for most of 2015'.

19 Brian Tracy, op. cit.

20 'To listen is better than anything, thus is born perfect love' – Ptahhotep, from Christian Jacq, *The Living Wisdom of Ancient Egypt*, Simon & Schuster (1999).

21 William James, 'the deepest principle of human nature is the craving to be appreciated'; note the word 'craving'. Not 'need' or 'desire', but craving: it truly is a human addiction.

22 Reaction tends to be thoughtless; what we want is a response, which is more considered.

23 One reason for this in the UK is that, up until the abolition of so-called O' Level English Language certification in 1988, paraphrasing – or précis as it was called as a

written exercise – was a standard and important part of the examination. The succeeding GCSE type exam abandoned this essential skill; clearly, it was thought too difficult! Précis, strictly understood, requires an exact understanding of the original, whereas paraphrasing suggests a looser grasp of what is intended by the speaker or writer.

24 Richard Brimble with Martin Clark, *Keeping the Human Factor Alive in the Digital Age*, Understanding and Learning Ltd (2006).
25 Peter Drucker, *Adventures of a Bystander* (1998).
26 Richard Brimble, op cit.

Chapter 3

Motivation, communication and relationships

In Chapter 2 we said that we would return to certain thematic preoccupations underpinning all effective motivation and engagement strategies, and explicitly one of these is communication. In fact, the concept of communication can scarcely be downplayed in any organisation, team or community of human beings. All depends upon effective communication. On a personal level it's estimated that 15% of our earning potential comes from knowledge and direct skills we possess, whereas 85% results from our interpersonal and leadership skills.[1] This is a huge disparity from what we expect and are taught to believe; after all, we have traditionally tended to blithely accept that if we do well at school and college and get 'qualifications', then our future career is assured. How palpably false this might be is now more than ever evident as record numbers of young people graduate and find, except in a small raft of subjects, there are no relevant jobs waiting for them. And the same sort of statistic is true at organisational level: some 85% of success is attributable to communication.[2] Effective communication, at root, is motivational, because by its very nature – if it is effective – it enables understanding, and ideally the understanding is not just intellectual assent (that is, in the mind, the head), but affects the emotions (heart) and the body (gut) too. To affect the heart, of course, is to generate desire – motivation – and to affect the body is to generate motion, which means actual and specific behaviours.

We looked in Figure 1.4 at the performance pyramid of Motivational Maps. To remind ourselves, it is shown again in Figure 3.1.

This model of performance is accurate – given the further refinements described in Chapter 1 – and relevant to both individuals and organisations. But what if a small, almost imperceptible, re-arrangement of the ordering here were to have massive implications for engagement? And such we find things to be: if we re-arrange our performance pyramid as shown in Figure 3.2 we find all the difference in the world.

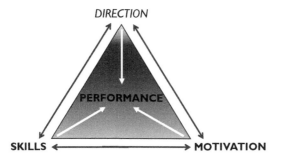

Figure 3.1 Performance pyramid for direction

Figure 3.2 Performance pyramid for engagement

Activity 3.1

Compare Figures 3.1 and 3.2. What is the difference between them? And why do you think this is so? What reasons do you think might explain this difference and why might it be significant?

The starting point for nearly every organisation, and individual, is invariably direction: what is our direction or organisational strategy, or what is my career path going to be? Keep in mind, then, the personal application of this argument, and that what we are about to say about organisations applies at an individual level too. The organisation decides that there is a gap in the market for, say, this innovative product, or this cheaper service, or this quicker customer or consumer outcome (DIRECTION), and from this analysis and breakdown it decides it needs a certain number of employees who have the specific skills and knowledge (SKILLS) to make that possible to deliver. Then, with those two performance imperatives in place, they employ people and either assume they will be motivated because they have a job, or hope that the package they are offering them will motivate them to make that discretionary effort that is the hallmark of engagement (MOTIVATION). In this sequence of events, therefore, which we think from our experience is typical, there is a clear order and hierarchy of importance; and in this hierarchy motivation is the least important aspect of the performance formula, since it seems to appear as an afterthought – something tagged on at the end, as it were.

But if we now turn this round and start with motivation as our cornerstone, then we get a very different kind of organisation. Here, if we start with motivation, then we are starting with 'why' we do what we do; we are checking in on the hearts and minds of the individuals involved. Indeed, it asks us to be clear about our purpose, not some imposed, extraneous and arbitrary purpose (which usually means one uniform thing: making money, which is not a purpose but a result), but a purpose – a 'why' – that is something intrinsic to us, and so deeply motivating. As Daniel Pink[3] put it: motivation acts as a 'purpose maximiser'. The direction we are going in does not express our purpose, but tells us more about 'what' we are doing and where that leads us to (a result); our skills and knowledge manifestly tells us about 'how' we are doing what we are doing. But Simon Sinek[4] said, 'WHAT companies do are external factors, but WHY they do it is something deeper'; and that something deeper links to our motivators.[5]

If we look at the nine motivators this becomes very transparent (Figure 3.3), because a whole language of purpose is contained in the nine motivators.

Searcher	to make a difference	... to lives, to communities, to the world
Spirit	to be free	... from hassle, from constraint, from limitations
Creator	to create and improve	... new products, new services, new ideas
Expert	to learn and teach	... skills, knowledge, insights
Builder	to compete	... against rivals, against standards and measures, to be the best
Director	to control	... people, resources, futures and destinies
Star	to impress and be appreciated by	... others, power-brokers and VIPs, hierarchies
Friend	to experience	... friendship, belonging to a group, community
Defender	to be secure and future-proofed	... through planning, processes, procedures

Figure 3.3 Motivators and purposes

Activity 3.2

Whereas it would be true to say that any motivator could be applicable to any organisation anywhere, nevertheless it is also obvious that some types of organisation clearly focus on one specific motivator as the basis for their purpose. To take an obvious example, not all schools will have a central purpose to 'learn and teach', but many will; just as football clubs will mainly want to 'compete' – that is their purpose, to win matches (with exceptions, as for example, a charity team where there may be another purpose).

Go through the list of nine purposes and ask yourself, what type of organisation or activity are you most likely to associate with each motivator?[6] Having done that, move from the generic – a school might be your example of 'expert' – to the specific: do you know of a particular school where the overt mission statement makes reference to this purpose? Once you have done this, you may be in a position to see more clearly how important the choice of purpose is, and how it is vital to choose a true purpose, both for the organisation and for its employees who ultimately need to buy into it.

Two important points emerge as preliminaries from this account so far. The first is that if motivators and purposes need to be closely aligned, then it is a matter of some import that we not only consider how employees individually relate to the organisation's purpose, but how the organisational motivational profile does too. This is where we can consider the Organisational Motivational Map,[7] which aggregates all the individual scores, and produces a ranked order of what motivates the organisation overall. Here what is significant is whether the overt purpose is really reinforced by the employees collectively.

In Figure 3.4, a sample of the company's Organisational Motivational Map is shown using four teams from its HQ. From it we can clearly see that the employees across the board want:

To make a difference – so serve customers meaningfully;
To learn and teach – so be involved in serious professional development; and
To be secure and future-proofed – so have solid plans and effective processes.

The organisation's actual mission statement starts: 'to reinvent the way in which people purchase "x" in the UK' (amended to preserve confidentiality). So, without rushing to judgement, these motivators may be relevant: 'the way' suggests a process (suiting Defender), the 'people' changing suggests a difference (suiting Searcher), and the capability to do this may well involve expertise (suiting Expert). However, we may equally be concerned that the word 'reinvent' might predicate Creator (currently ranked only 5th in the Organisational Map – Figure 3.4) being higher, but this depends, perhaps, on the sector, which is a wider issue.

But also note, in the Organisational Motivational Map, the 'PMA Rank' scores. We see that for this organisation, the Searcher is the most important

Team Name	Searcher	Expert	Defender	Director	Creator	Spirit	Builder	Star	Friend	Motivation Audit %
Customer Service	251	250	198	162	166	139	155	167	132	82%
Admin	222	180	197	120	154	137	139	133	158	71%
Managers	241	180	193	211	160	168	159	170	138	75%
Directors	82	64	62	56	62	83	61	37	33	90%
Scoring Totals	796	674	650	549	542	527	514	507	461	77%
PMA Total	233	232	224	214	213	213	184	201	230	
PMA %	80%	80%	77%	74%	73%	73%	63%	69%	79%	
PMA Rank	1	2	4	5	6	7	9	8	3	

dark grey - 1st motivator

middle grey - 2nd motivator

light grey - 3rd motivator

textured grey - lowest motivator

Figure 3.4 Organisational Motivational Map

motivator (its scoring total is 796); but we also see from the PMA Rank of 1 (80%) – that is, 1st – that the employees are most satisfied with it! Which means that the motivator, Searcher, is the motivator most important (or valuable) for the employees AND at the same time the one they feel that is most satisfied by their work or organisation. However, the levels of current satisfaction do not exactly mirror the rankings of all the motivators. For example, and very noticeably, Friend is the least important motivator, ranked 9th, but it is 3rd in terms of satisfaction rating. What does this mean? It means, almost certainly, that although belonging and teams are relatively unimportant to employees, the management or the structure creates a good sense of belonging anyway. So that indicates good management. Less happy, though, is the Builder motivator: employees have ranked money and material possessions 7th – so again, not critical to their serious concerns – except that in terms of their satisfaction it is 9th. In other words, this organisation – staff feel – is underpaying them for what they provide. Given that Builder is only 7th in terms of their order of importance, then this probably is not going to undermine the stability of the organisation by – for example – high staff turnover (which indeed it doesn't), but imagine the consequences if their number one motivator, Searcher, was also 9th in the PMA Rank order, how organisationally critical that might be: it would mean that the motivator staff most want is the one they feel they are getting the least. That would almost certainly mean total disengagement looming ahead.

Our second point about the motivators and purposes is that it inevitably links us to the first MacLeod imperative for engagement: namely, the strategic narrative. You will remember that in Chapter 2 we also referred to this as being intimately linked to 'visible, empowering leadership'; indeed, it can scarcely not be. Bookshops are full of texts about lessons to be learnt from the most successful organisations in the world, and invariably these all have empowering leadership and leaders who have a tale to tell. For example, Walt Disney and Disney, Steve Jobs and Apple, Bill Gates and Microsoft, Richard Branson and Virgin, James Dyson and Dyson, Jeff Bezos and Amazon, and one could go on. These companies represent some of the very biggest in the world, but the same principle applies all the way down the organisational chain. For, if we look at smaller companies in the UK, we find fascination at how the Innocent drinks company came to be,[8] or how Jo Malone[9] became the 'English scent maverick' and set up Jo Loves, and so on. Their stories are compelling. One reason why is given explicitly in the title of James Dyson's book: *Against the Odds: An Autobiography.*[10] We all like underdogs – heroes and heroines who fought against tremendous odds, difficulties and resistance, but prevailed anyway. We all face difficulties and challenges in our life, and narratives that surmount them help enable us. Thus, these stories inspire us, and we want to get a 'bit of that action' for ourselves, as readers, and yes, as employees too. For as employees there is a certain cachet in being 'part' of the big narrative; it fills us with significance – we too are helping realise a higher, transcendental purpose. One can never underestimate how important this is – and how profoundly engaging.

Thus, every strategic narrative is going to be unique, forged in the fire of the personal circumstances and environment of each leader or founder or entrepreneur who strives to deliver their vision of what the future looks like for them. This means there is no *one* template, for if there were the purpose would be inauthentic, merely a copy of someone else's.[11] But what we can more directly address in terms of engagement is the 'visible, empowering leadership' that is the core aspect of having the strategic narrative. Why? Because the strategic narrative is redundant unless it is communicated. To communicate is to make 'visible' that story which is underpinning the enterprise or the organisation. In making it 'visible', then – and if it is authentic – we begin that process of empowering employees[12] to identify with it, and so to contribute to it. Which is: to engage.

Let's be clear, however, before returning to the word 'visible', the task of leadership is, as Sir John Harvey Jones suggested, 'to make remaining in the status quo more risky than launching into the new unknown'.[13] Communicating the strategic narrative clearly and effectively to employees, which of course outlines the situation – crisis even – which precipitated the initial organisational purpose, and leads on to its future resolution, or the vision of the promised land where we want to be, by its very nature reduces risk because it creates an easily understandable picture in the mind. This, again, is compelling.

And here we need to look at that wonderful word 'visible' in more detail. Because visible, strictly understood, refers to the organ of sight. However, when we talk about the leader communicating in an empowering way, we are not just referring to the 'visible' as being something that is in our line of sight.

Activity 3.3

What are the ways in which we might communicate, other than visually? Make a list. What might be the drawbacks of only communicating visually? Wherever you work, including in your own business or organisation, what different ways do you use to communicate, and how many different ways are being used to communicate with you? Which are effective?

According to neuro-linguistic programming[14] there are four major styles of communication (Figure 3.5),[15] and if we wish to build more rapport with people – with our employees – we need to communicate with them in their preferred style of communication. Unfortunately, organisations and corporations tend to communicate in one monotonous and uniform style, which is sadly the AD or Auditory Digital style. We say sadly because this style can only be a first preference[16] for a small minority of the population at best, which means that in any large organisation, apart from any other factors disrupting communications, the large majority of the employees are not really going to get the messages, much less the strategic narrative.

Getting your message across, then, requires in the first instance rapport,[17] of which probably the most critical element is developing listening skills – indeed, not just a skill but a mind-set wholly dedicated to 'tuning' in to what other people are saying. This of course requires intense practice and determination, and we have covered five aspects of how to improve listening in Chapter 2. This requirement cannot be stressed enough, since it is not enough to engage with VAK and other techniques and think they are going to work without this primary requirement to listen. But given that, we now come to a process that, if we think it through, can have a profound effect on how we communicate with, and so lead, our employees.

Basically, most corporate – and organisational and company – communication is transmitted through AD, or Auditory Digital style. This is unfortunate, although ostensibly there is a very compelling reason why this is so. Auditory Digital[18] style means that messages are communicated in terms of the relevant facts and figures.

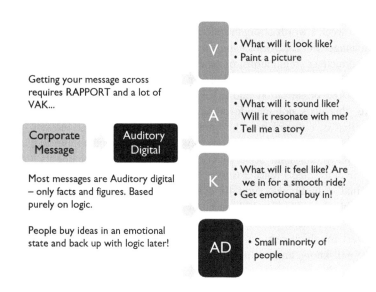

Figure 3.5 Four major styles of communicating: VAK + AD

Activity 3.4

Why do you think that it is unfortunate that most corporate communication is carried out in AD style? And what compelling reasons might there be for this situation to have arisen? Make a note of your answers before reading on.

It is unfortunate because it does not excite or motivate or inspire the vast majority of the employees! And the compelling reasons why this situation has arisen is blindingly simple: on the one hand, it is because writing in the AD style is the easiest, most efficient, most time effective (but of course not in the long run) way of writing; and on the other hand, all organisations tend to be time poor. There is too much to do in too little time, change initiatives are always sprouting like dandelions on a wet lawn, and so we must get to the point – the heart of the matter – as soon as possible; for if we don't we feel as if we are wasting time. And, after all, what more do we need than the facts and figures? In its own AD style it makes sense to think like this: it's logical, isn't it?

It is logical but it's wrong! There is a wealth of evidence now that backs up the old fable that it is the tortoise that wins the race, not the speeding hare. Slow, in fact, can be good.[19] Thus we need to review how we communicate with employees at a fundamental level. First, then, ask yourself how do you, or the organisation you work for, communicate with employees?

Activity 3.5

Consider a week's worth of organisational communications. Break them down into easily manageable categories: spoken (one-2-one, team meeting); paper-based (memos, directives, regulations, or other); and electronic (emails, intranets, social media, or other). Keep in mind here we are looking at how the organisation (or you, if you are the organisation and so in charge) communicates with employees; therefore, this does not include communication to organisational customers or clients – that is, outward bound communications – since these are not the issue here, although clearly the implications of what we are saying applies to these too.

What is the dominant style of communication in each category? And, on balance, overall? See Figure 3.6 to help you assemble this information.

The final column asks you to evaluate how 'effective' in each area the communication is. This could be a number – out of 10 where 10 is high – or a qualitative assessment. Either way, if one is a manager, then one may not know the answer! In which case: ask. Ask the recipients of the communication. They certainly will know, and will tell you if approached in the right way.

Activity 3.6

Having done this analysis, the question now becomes: how do we improve our internal communications to employees? Given that there is almost certainly too much AD style communication, the issue becomes one of increasing the

TYPE OF COMMUNICATION	SUB-TYPE	VAK or AD	TIME SPENT	%OF TIME SPENT	EFFECTIVENESS
SPEECH	1-2-1				
	In teams				
	Meetings				
	Other				
PAPER	Memos				
	Directives				
	Regulations				
	Other				
ELECTRONIC	Emails				
	Intranets				
	Social media				
	Other				

Figure 3.6 Style of communication across organisation

percentage of VAK style materials. The starting point for engagement would be to consider your own organisation's strategic narrative – its purpose and how that is expressed.

Our/my strategic narrative is: here are some helpful ways of thinking about creating a more VAK friendly message (Figure 3.7).

'A PC in every home'[20]
'Everything you need is already inside ... Just Do It'[21]
'Men wanted ... in case of success'[22]

One extra thing you may notice about this VAK exercise, and thinking about your own organisation – as an employee or employer – is that its implications go way beyond just communicating effectively with the staff that we have. Indeed, when we think about it we see that creating these messages in this way also acts as a beacon or – to switch metaphors – a magnet to new recruits. The Shackleton example is a particularly good example, for it is quite obvious that for most people the advert is a turn-off: who, in their 'right' mind, wants that kind of job – 'safe return doubtful'? Perhaps Shackleton could have had far more applicants if he had down-played the danger and difficulties, talked up the

Figure 3.7 Increasing the VAK in communications

technical and nautical abilities required, or even the comradeship or important exploration that they were about to embark upon. But he didn't do that because he wanted a certain type of man, one for whom the dangers and difficulties were themselves (perversely, perhaps, from our perspective) the attraction. In short, he was creating an ethos, a culture, a team or blend of people who were under no illusions about what was to happen and why, and wanted that. Put another way, they were highly motivated upfront. Think about it – motivated towards facing life-threatening challenges!

Imagine the impact, then, of this on your organisation if you were able to recruit and retain just the kind of people who buy into your strategic narrative because you have communicated it much more effectively via VAK. And if we want to give you a good analogy for how this works in everyday life, then consider a really good restaurant you have been to. Yes, at some point you will get the auditory-visual messages on the menu, but it's not a 'really good' restaurant if that is all you have to rely on before you buy. No, as you walk in your senses should be stimulated: first, by the visuals (V) on the walls, the furniture and lighting; by the sounds (A), background sound effects (sometimes music) that subtly reinforce the ambience; thirdly, that smell (K) emanating from the kitchen that makes you salivate and feel like eating something; and finally, and critically, the warmth, enthusiasm and helpfulness of the waiter/ waitress who shows you to your seat. The perfect experience is when all these factors meet, you give your order, and the food then meets the high expectations that the VAK + AD have generated. And what does it all produce at the end of the day, or evening? Customer loyalty and retention; you want to go back and do it again. In the same way the employee, given the analogy at work, wants to get back to work to contribute more because the experience is so good.

Ultimately, the whole experience and the strategic narrative that conveys it represent the values that we stand for. The reason that many buying experiences are not overly pleasurable or consistent in their 'feel' is because the organisation has not systematically thought through its values: what it stands for as an organisation. For, as Bob Garrett expressed it, 'A Value is a belief in action'.[23] But what are our values?

Like the strategic narrative itself, your values will be yours individually. They will also be collectively – whether consciously or not –inherent in any team, and any organisation. The key thing is to identify them and make them explicit to you, and subsequently to the team and the whole organisation. Our forth-coming books, *Mapping Motivation for Management* and *Mapping Motivation for Strategy*,[24] cover team and organisational values in a lot more detail, but for now let's consider making an individual's values transparent.

Activity 3.7

Because 'values' like motivation are often invisible to the conscious mind (in the same way perhaps that we are always being affected physically by gravity, but rarely become aware that we are), then the best way to make them explicit is indirectly by considering something else. Write down your answers to these four questions.

1.   Which three people do you admire the most, and why?[25]
2.   Which three people don't you admire, and why?
3.   Name three organisations you admire, and why you admire them.
4.   Name three organisations you don't admire, and why not.

Having got your answers, this now requires that you drill down on the meaning of them. The 'why?' is critical. At this point one has to be personal in order to convey the significance of the data, but co-author James Sale might identify the following three people:

> *Jesus Christ – because … unshakeable purpose, extemporaneous ability to cope with any challenge, charismatic.*

> *William Shakespeare – because … huge ability yet self-effacing, creative poet but shrewd business man too, profound insight into human nature.*

> *My wife, Linda E Sale – because … deeply loving and loveable, loyal, creative and artist.*

In admiring these people for these qualities, what I am really saying is that these qualities are really deep values that I wish I could emulate and exhibit, or be *like*. So, to take the first person, Jesus Christ, and his perceived qualities from my perspective: I would like myself to show 'unshakeable purpose'; and it is important to me to be *able* – to cope with any situation and without preparation if necessary; and yes, to be charismatic – attractive through words and actions so that others voluntarily wish to follow me. Given that, then the kind of organisations I am going to like will reflect those qualities almost certainly; and, of course, I will be aversive to people and organisations which lack true purpose, which can't cope meaningfully with challenge and change, and which – frankly (from my perspective[26]) – are routine or boring.

The values, then, explicitly (for Jesus Christ) might be: determination/focus, flexibility/spontaneity, and inspiration/energy. This may require further 'drill down' to dig out the full implications of my choices, but clearly valuable information is emerging from this through which I can choose the right kind of organisation, business, activity or purpose for myself. Keep in mind here that I have only answered question one – a lot more will emerge with questions two to four, especially in identifying what is to be avoided.

To conclude this chapter let's return to the observation we made regarding using VAK communication styles in addition in the traditional AD style. We said that this would have an impact not only on existing employees and retaining them, but also on recruiting new ones as the power of the communication becomes a beacon or magnet to people outside the organisation. Mapping Motivation here has another unique role to play: recruitment.

Often when considering new employees, organisations resort to using psychometric tests which relate to personality and behaviours, and these can be useful. But the truth is: nobody goes to work on a Monday morning because of their personality or behaviour, as per their psychometric test. And one's personality does not really correlate with one's performance and productivity, anyway. It is true that for a small number of roles – for example, a fighter pilot – being a certain type of person is necessary. But the number of these 'roles' is relatively small. People go to work on a Monday morning because (or in spite) of their motivators, and it is their motivators that are correlated with their performance and productivity.

Thus, it is by using Motivational Maps in the recruitment process that we can more easily ascertain whether an individual is going to be a 'fit' into the team and the organisation, and further, whether the individual is, or is likely to be, engaged or not. These, of course, are big claims. We cannot cover the whole recruitment process here, but one aspect is crucial: namely, being aware that the number one factor in all high performance employees is high levels of energy.[27] Establishing this at the interview stage is absolutely crucial for a successful hire. As we all know, alas, many people are very high energy – at interview – but this does not translate into a high energy employee when they are given the job! Therefore, as all candidates with an ounce of common sense will claim to be high energy people, smart recruiters will attempt to drill down on the answers given to try to confirm that the energy is real, consistent and durable. This is a highly sophisticated process. But, since motivation is energy, then using the Motivational Maps can give any recruiter a huge head start when interviewing, especially the final short list of candidates. In Chapter 5 we show how Motivational Maps can be used by the engaging manager to acquire the best and most suitable candidates for any role within any organisation. But first, in Chapter 4, we turn to look at motivation and employee voice.

Notes

1 '15% of your earning potential comes from knowledge and direct skills … 85% comes from your leadership and interpersonal skills' – Dale Carnegie, cited in https://bit.ly/2EFbMbm.
2 Again, 'Research carried out by the Carnegie Institute of Technology shows that 85 percent of your financial success is due to skills in "human engineering," your personality and ability to communicate, negotiate, and lead. Shockingly, only 15 percent is due to technical knowledge.' Keld Jensen, cited in Forbes, http://bit.ly/2yqIvz7 12th April, 2012. Quite a lot of effort online has been put into debunking this statistic and questioning its provenance; our own view would be that its general acceptance is due to the fact that it is probably true, despite its seeming counter-intuitive nature. The kind of mind-set that wants to debunk the statistic seems to us exactly the kind of mind-set that wishes to continue predicating technology as more important than people: the old twentieth century way, in fact.

3 Daniel Pink, *Drive*, Canongate (2010).

4 Simon Sinek, *Start with Why*, Penguin (2009).

5 Sinek's first example of the power of 'why' is Apple Inc. In brief he explains how instead of positioning the company as a 'what' company – what we do is make great computers – instead, they position themselves as a 'why' company – why we exist is to challenge the status quo and make beautifully designed, simple to use and user-friendly products, and hey, one of these happens to be a great computer. By doing so, they enter a unique marketing space.

6 So, for example (and of course not solely including), Searcher: charities; Spirit: space exploration (as an extreme example!); Creator: technology; Expert: medicine; Builder: sport; Director: the military; Star: media organisations; Friend: project/team based companies; Defender: public services. Specific but hypothetical examples might be: Searcher: Oxfam; Spirit: Space X; Creator: Apple Inc.; Expert: Royal Marsden Hospital Cancer Research; Builder: Manchester United; Director: The British Army; Star: Walt Disney; Friend: Accenture; Defender: The Civil Service. Please keep in mind that these are just examples. The Creator (and all nine motivators) applies across a much broader range than just technology – consider the arts, the performing arts and so on; but we hope the gist is clear.

7 The Organisational Motivational Map is a development of the Motivational Map, created by James Sale, and available from Motivational Maps Limited and its senior practitioners.

8 Richard Reed, http://bit.ly/1vx8bQo. This company was so successful, 90% of it was bought by Coca-Cola.

9 Jo Malone, *Jo Malone: My Story*, Simon & Schuster (2017).

10 Orion Business Books (1997).

11 And this of course is why some organisations fail before they even start: for they start by simply copying other organisations' purposes (and ideas); ultimately even large corporates can fail when the initial purpose that drove them to succeed becomes diluted and they become indistinguishable from every other corporate. What we like to call 'me-too' organisations.

12 Employees first, but of course there is a marketing application here, for ultimately the customers and clients get to identify with the story, which ultimately becomes part of the 'brand' of the company.

13 Cited by John Kotter in the Harvard Business Review, May–June, 1995.

14 Three of these, VAK, are also covered in our companion volume: *Mapping Motivation for Coaching*, James Sale and Bevis Moynan, Routledge (2018), Chapter 4.

15 Less important from an organisational point of view, and so not major from our perspective here, are the senses of smell (olfactory) and taste (gustatory), which are also ways in which we can communicate with others.

16 There are various complications in establishing exactly what percentage of the population might have Visual, or Auditory or Kinaesthetic or Auditory Digital as their dominant perceptual mode (and of course people can switch to a secondary preference); but if we consider that the figure of 60% for Visual is often cited, then AD is clearly not a majority preferred mode. See https://bit.ly/1gfiKFM.

17 For more on building rapport and NLP see *Mapping Motivation for Coaching*, as above.

18 Auditory Digital is sometimes referred to as 'self-talk' and because it is an 'inner dialogue', it tends to be more abstract than sensuous. So people preferring this style will tend to use abstract words and more complicated sentences; they will also emphasise logic and 'what makes sense' to them. See Harry Alder and Beryl Heather, *NLP in 21 Days*, Piatkus (1999) for more on this fascinating topic.

19 The most well-known research adopting this position is *In Praise of Slow* by Carl Honoré, Orion Books (2004). The epigraph, citing Gandhi, says it all: 'There is more

to life than increasing its speed'. Other good books that advance a similar argument within various contexts include: Guy Claxton, *Hare Brain, Tortoise Mind*, Fourth Estate (1997), and Timothy Ferriss' *The Four-Hour Work Week*, Crown Publishers (2007).

20 Bill Gates of Microsoft as early as 1980 said, 'A computer on every desk and in every home'. In one phrase that depicts a very clear picture.

21 Cited by Jonah Sachs in *Winning the Story Wars*, Harvard Business Review Press (2012), this of course refers to the astonishing traction of Nike's marketing campaigns that have resonated throughout the world. People everywhere have made the story of 'just doing it' their own.

22 This is the astonishing advert that Ernest Shackleton put out looking for recruits to his extraordinary Antarctic expedition in 1914, which has to be ranked as one of the greatest expeditions in human history. It is disputed whether the advert actually appeared, or whether in fact it was some story in the newspapers about the expedition that provoked applicants to apply. But, allegedly, there were some 5,000 applications for the 27 crew posts on the ship.

23 Bob Garrett, *The Fish Rots from the Head*, Harper Collins (1997).

24 To be published by Routledge in 2019 and 2020 respectively.

25 And to be clear, the three people may be real, living or dead, or even imaginary – a character from a book, for example Gandalf in *The Lord of the Rings*!

26 Properly understood, nothing of course is boring; if we think so, we simply do not know enough or have not considered it properly. Whenever, for example, we encounter and have to sit through a truly boring speaker, then even here the interest is: why is this speaker so boring and so ineffective? What can I learn from mediocrity?

27 This is almost self-evident, since clearly a lack of energy, no matter what the talent or skills, is bound to lead to lacklustre performances. But for a compelling and full account of this, see Lou Adler, *Hire with Your Head: A Rational Way to Make a Gut Reaction*, Wiley (1998).

Chapter 4

Motivation and finding the employee voice

One of the reasons why engagement is popular with HR and in organisational literature is that it is, allegedly, 'measurable'. Indeed, the MacLeod Report makes that very point. But whilst being measurable is a good thing, because then we can view the effects of our actions to improve things, one still has to ask the question: given its measurability, why hasn't employee engagement significantly improved in the 20 or so years since this concept went mainstream? Many commentators have noted this phenomenon.[1]

Perhaps the reason is that what is being measured is not really the right determinant, and the way in which it is being measured – invariably through a 'staff survey' – is also not the optimum way to do the measuring. This latter point – how it is being measured – is relevant here because we are going to address the issue of 'employee voice', the third strand, according to MacLeod, of employee engagement. It would seem obvious that by having a staff survey – inviting staff to comment on their impressions of the organisation – we are at the very heart of employee engagement: what could be more engaging than listening to the employee's voice? And we would agree that it is better to have a staff survey – at least one that is well constructed – than not to have one. But our point is, it's probably not optimum, and there is a much better way to get at whether or not staff are engaged, via Motivational Maps. Naturally, it requires a little more thought, a little more understanding, than simply distributing a staff survey and reading off the results, but the extra care and attention – and the insight it thus generates – is worth it, as we hope to show. But first, why do we think that staff surveys are not optimum and not the way to go in the long term?

Activity 4.1

What do you think the benefits of a staff survey are? If you have experienced or administered one, how did you find it and/or the outcomes deriving from it? And what do you think the downsides of a staff survey might be? List and rank in order the three most important for you.

Different organisations may have differing views on what is beneficial about staff surveys, but we think three really important ones are, firstly, to measure satisfaction with specific work-related issues: job satisfaction, pay packages and benefits, company policies, staff retention, working conditions and so on. Secondly, surveys can help identify strengths as well as areas of engagement that may be in need of enhancement, for example, role clarity, accountability, communication, personal and team recognition and relationships generally. Finally, but not exhaustively, surveys can be very useful for reviewing the whole organisation, particularly when there are large and serious changes afoot, like restructuring or mergers.

This sounds all good, which it is, but there are significant downsides. First, it is relatively expensive for what it is; after all, you would think that since staff have managers who are paid to manage them we might know what staff think and feel from the managers. In small organisations they sometimes do know (so why don't managers in large organisations, as they are generally paid more?). Put another way, it seems a form of managerial disempowerment. This is doubly the case, since often external consultants are brought in to administer and interpret the results. Second, the survey is 'obvious' in what it is seeking to know and establish. By which we mean the questions lack subtlety and can easily be manipulated.[2] This means staff can point score, promote agendas, and more generally dis-inform management of the real situation, real concerns, and the actual needs of the organisation. Third, the information by its nature can be fragmentary and not easy to implement and respond to. Indeed, one of the frequent criticisms of staff surveys by staff is that it is done and nothing subsequently happens or changes. This issue is related to MacLeod's fourth enabler, organisational integrity, one aspect of which must be walking the talk, or being consistent in behaviours. The point about the 'fragmentary' nature of the information is this: the more limited the survey is, the more focused the result, but also of course the more limited that result is by definition; the broader the scope of the survey, then the more diffuse and sometimes confusing the outcomes, and also the longer the time it takes to complete – which itself impacts individual productivity, and so is another cost. But a final issue here concerning broad brush staff surveys is the difficulty of employees to understand them sufficiently: the literacy, comprehension and capabilities of employees will necessarily be wide-ranging. Thus, as the survey extends its scope, and seeks to cover more areas of organisational interest, it will almost certainly increase in linguistic complexity. Given the average attention span is short, there is every chance that many submissions will not truly reflect the thinking of the participant.

Motivational Maps, however, are different.

Activity 4.2

What do you think the benefits of using Motivational Maps might be compared with using a staff survey? If you have not done a Map yet, go to the end of the Introduction to this book to find out how you can access one.

Unlike a staff survey, Motivational Maps are relatively inexpensive to implement; one reason for this of course is that they never need to be bespoke. They are what they are and their use and usefulness is universal. That's quite different from having to create a staff survey and agonise over the wording to ensure it covers all the bases, and is in a language suitable for the espoused values of the organisation. So, a corollary benefit of this point is that Maps are far faster to implement and understand; there is therefore a time saving too.

Second, and paradoxically, Maps are subtle, and reveal both specifics and trends, despite the fact that the language of the diagnostic tool is actually simple to understand, and is standardised (via sentence stems) in very specific ways that make it easy to grasp. Thus, what is revealed is not obvious. We talk of making the 'invisible' visible.[3] But although not obvious, the information can be readily understood and can be immediately acted upon. It also has a direct bearing on the staff and the teams in a way that no staff survey can – for the Map knows what people really want! And this must always be a matter of serious interest to the effective leader. Indeed, we have found in fact that it is only effective leaders who want to embrace this technology; weak, ineffective leaders are frightened of it, because actually finding out what your employees really want – as opposed to ticking boxes – is really letting the genie out of the bottle! So, this is not a form of management disempowerment either, because what the Maps reveal no-one could reasonably expect a manager to know, though once known, it becomes extremely actionable and practical.

Finally, the individual Map tells us what the individual wants; the Motivational Team Map tells us what the team collectively wants, and it also points towards potential conflicts (conflicting energy directions) within the team that might derail it from its remit. The more recent organisational Map takes mapping to another level: it tells us what each team wants, and also what collectively the whole organisation wants. One needs to grasp at this point that when a large number of people are profiled the collective effect of the motivators is more or less now equivalent to measuring the 'values' within the organisation. Why is this significant? Because we can now begin to see whether the espoused values – and its translation into mission and vision statements – are really reflected in the aspirations of the staff. If they are not, then a major problem looms ahead, and one which needs immediate attention. And further, that immediate attention can itself be addressed through the Maps' own reward strategies, which is to say, giving employees what they are likely to want.

On all the criteria, then, Motivational Maps are superior to the staff survey. But how might this look in practical terms, keeping in mind that we are specifically considering 'employee voice' here? Let's consider for starters three pieces of Motivational Map information (Figure 4.1) which are directly related to 'employee voice'.

First, the Map Personal Motivational Audit (PMA) scores on an individual basis, as well as team and organisational scores.

Name	Expert	Searcher	Spirit	Defender	Creator	Builder	Director	Friend	Star	Personal Motivation	1	2	3
Richard	22	22	21	23	19	19	16	21	17	80%	7	10	9
Keith	18	20	19	20	19	19	22	20	23	34%	1	9	1
John	28	18	26	22	21	15	22	11	17	86%	10	5	8
Sajid	21	18	32	16	27	21	31	5	9	88%	8	10	10
Clive	30	35	10	25	25	15	18	13	9	10%	1	1	1
Amanda	26	27	25	22	16	26	5	25	8	62%	6	8	5
Total	145	140	133	128	127	115	114	95	83	66%			

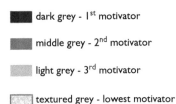

dark grey - 1st motivator

middle grey - 2nd motivator

light grey - 3rd motivator

textured grey - lowest motivator

Figure 4.1 Team Map with individual scores

Activity 4.3

Study this Team Motivational Map. What issues in it can you identify that might have a bearing on engagement issues?

To be clear: in allowing employees to complete a Motivational Map we are enabling their voice to be heard – assuming of course that we don't discount that voice by ignoring the results of their Map. What we are saying to them is that what you want at a deep psychological level is important to us, and we want to hear this and to act upon it.

Motivation is not engagement; it is a subset of it. Engagement is (motivation + behaviours). But the core component is the motivation since it drives the behaviours, not the other way round. Thus, the first thing to notice is each individual's motivational score, for this is telling us how energised they are at work.

On the face of it, then, what would we say? Certainly, Sajid is highly motivated, and so highly likely to be engaged. Conversely, Clive is poorly motivated and so highly likely to be disengaged. The high range of the scores – 76 points (86 minus 10) – suggests that the team is not functioning as a team, and that certainly management is not yet effective in dealing with Clive.[4]

Now consider the Motivation Audit scores and what they are telling us; this is crucial. Let's take three stark examples from the team and expand what this means, and how it links to engagement and the 'voice' of the employee.

Activity 4.4

Figure 4.3 should make clearer what the issues are here about employees, what they are feeling, and what their 'voice' is telling us. Before reading on, make

SAJID	86% motivated	highest motivation
AVERAGE FOR TEAM	66% motivated	turning point for team: below? above?
CLIVE	10% motivated	lowest motivation

Figure 4.2 Two people and the average to consider in a team

SATISFACTION FEELINGS ACROSS TOP 3 MOTIVATORS			
	No 1 Motivator	No 2 Motivator	No 3 Motivator	
Keith	Star 1/10	Director 9/10	Friend 1/10	34%
John	Expert 10/10	Spirit 5/10	Director 8/10	86%
Clive	Searcher 1/10	Expert 1/10	Defender 1/10	10%

Figure 4.3 Exploring employee voice at work

some notes about what you think Keith, John and Clive's results mean: what are their voices individually telling us?

Keep in mind that any comment we make needs to contextualised and verified either by talking to Keith or Keith's manager. But Keith seems to be telling us that he is demotivated, and this is primarily because his top motivator, Star, or the need for recognition, is being wholly unmet. He has scored that 1/10 in terms of satisfaction. Equally, his third most important motivator, the Friend, the need to belong, is also only 1/10. So what we have is an employee who is saying, 'I don't feel recognised in my job and I don't feel I belong here either'. However, they are also saying, 'but in terms of the control I have over my work and colleagues, I feel great – I feel 9/10 about that! Wow!' So Keith is probably not trying just to send a negative message with his 1/10 scores, because when things are good – as in his control levels – he acknowledges that. The question, then, becomes for Keith (assuming he is a valuable member of staff we wish to retain): how can we as an organisation specifically increase his sense of recognition first and foremost; and secondly, how can we make him feel he belongs more and identifies with his team?

Activity 4.5

What are your top three tips – if you were his manager – for giving Keith more recognition in his work place? What generic ideas can you come up with that you think might meet this specific motivator?

The answer to how can we make Keith feel more recognised or appreciated in his role is answered by Motivational Maps via its reward strategies. These strategies appear in all the Map reports – individual, team and organisational – but each report only contains a limited number of them: somewhere between three and five for any given motivator. But this is simply scratching the surface, for consultants working in this field have something approaching 200 ideas to choose from, to advise the individual, or the manager, or the whole organisation. But let's look first at how this appears in an actual report. What were Keith's actual suggestions from his Map (Figure 4.4) – that is to say, things for him to attempt to do?

These are all relatively simple ideas and very 'do-able': by 'clarifying your qualifications' or by considering targets more aligned with 'high visibility', or by simply creating your own 'business card' you are taking steps to managing your own image and how you are perceived; you are increasing the chances of your being noticed – of you being a 'star', and so feeding your Star motivator. And what Keith does for his 'Star' can be done for any and all the motivators. But further than this we can – using Motivational Maps extended Reward Strategies Packs – consider what the manager can do to feed the Star motivator for their team member.

Clearly, one major aspect of the Star motivator is the desire for high prestige and this is most obviously associated with awards. Retail food outlets, for example, give five-star awards, hotels have employee of the month, and the basic

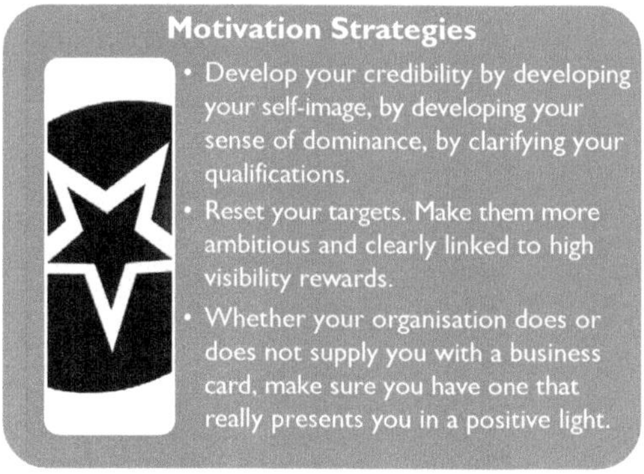

Figure 4.4 Keith's Star reward strategies from his Map

principle is sound in both examples. As Napoleon said, 'I cannot get a man to die for money, but I can get him to die for a medal'. What 'medals' can you award in your organisation? The key thing about awards from the management perspective is to make them little and often. It is better to have 12 small awards distributed 12 times throughout the year than one mega-award given only once.

So, if the Star wants PRESTIGE, consider the ideas in Figure 4.5.

A central point here, which especially applies to the Star motivator but also more generally across the board, is that people need to feel valued if they are to become engaged and give that discretionary effort that they normally withhold. The kind of things we are suggesting for the Star motivated individual also may have an application to other employees too; it's contextual and it depends, but in working out what is best for your employees and your organisation, it is advisable to think big about the small things, or incremental improvements that you can make.

Obviously, the process we have followed here we can replicate with Keith's other motivators. In the case of his second motivator, the Director, his satisfaction score is 9/10, so he is well satisfied currently with it. There is therefore a high likelihood that we do not need to address the issue of 'control' for Keith. But the motivator Friend, his third motivator, definitely does need addressing, as he has scored this 1/10, so he does not feel he belongs. But here the subtlety of the Maps comes into play, for if we consider both 'distressed' motivators at the same time, we realise that there may be a conflict internally for Keith. After all, the desire to be recognised – to be a 'star' as it were – sits uneasily with the desire to belong, to be 'one of the lads or lasses'. To be a star necessitates elevation above others; others can accept that within a team where they feel it is justified, but if Keith is the only person who needs this motivator fulfilled, and insists on it overtly or covertly as the case may be, then other team members may well come to feel devalued if this recognition is granted at their expense.

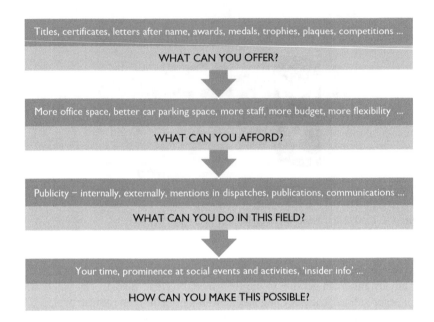

Titles, certificates, letters after name, awards, medals, trophies, plaques, competitions ...

WHAT CAN YOU OFFER?

More office space, better car parking space, more staff, more budget, more flexibility ...

WHAT CAN YOU AFFORD?

Publicity – internally, externally, mentions in dispatches, publications, communications ...

WHAT CAN YOU DO IN THIS FIELD?

Your time, prominence at social events and activities, 'insider info' ...

HOW CAN YOU MAKE THIS POSSIBLE?

Figure 4.5 Providing more recognition and prestige

Looking at Figure 4.1 we see that Keith is only person in the team with this motivator. In short, there is a motivational conflict that may be at the root of Keith's motivation.

There is another factor – or subtlety – as well that the team Map (Figure 4.1) reveals: look at the range of scores for Keith, his lowest is 18/40 and his highest is 23/40 (a range of 5 points), compared with, say, Clive, whose lowest score is 9/40 and highest 35/40 (a range of 26 points). All of Keith's motivators oscillate around the middle 20 (the maximum is 40) number. Put another way, quite apart from the fact that two of his top three motivators potentially drive him to want competing things, the range of his scores suggests balance rather than focus. Clive passionately wants and *craves* his Searcher or 'make a difference' motivator (35/40), which means much more focus on it, but Keith only *wants* his recognition or Star motivator, and the need to belong is scored equally[5] (20/40) with two other motivators. So what this is suggesting is that Keith may be difficult to motivate because:

a. He has conflicting motivators in his top three – the more he gets recognition, the less perhaps others accept him and the less he belongs; conversely the more he belongs to the team and accepts his role as being just one of them, the less recognition he may get.

b. His motivational intensity – focus – is not strong, and so all motivators virtually come into play. His lowest motivator, the Expert (18/40), means that he is not averse to training or learning, although it doesn't particularly motivate him either.

We come back then to realising that in order to motivate and engage Keith more we need to use this information contextually – by discussing with Keith some of the issues we have outlined above. This, of course, is really giving Keith – the employee – a voice. It is going in at a level that is profound and meaningful for him. But the Maps can go further still, and in this case – that is, given the complexity and contradictions in the motivational profile – they would. For whenever there is internal motivational conflict or lack of motivational focus through a narrow scoring range we need not only to look at the team numbers but to go deeper into the individual Map, Keith's individual map.

This now becomes an 'advanced' case study – the kind of thing that only deep training in reading Maps can produce. As a shorthand we sometimes refer to it as, 'reading the 22 numbers' (Figure 4.6).

This information is essentially an extension of listening to the employee's voice, for what we are seeing is not only how satisfied Keith is with his top three motivators, but how he feels about all the motivators, whether they motivate him or not.

Analysis for Keith: Raw Results

Motivator	Score	PMA Score / 10
Star	23	1
Director	22	9
Friend	20	1
Defender	20	1
Searcher	20	9
Builder	19	1
Spirit	19	1
Creator	19	1
Expert	18	8
PMA Score	34%	
Cluster Importance		
Relationship (R)	35%	
Achievement (A)	33%	
Growth (G)	32%	

Figure 4.6 Keith's 22 numbers

Activity 4.6

Study the numbers in the PMA column. Keep in mind that they refer to how well –
as a score out of 10 – the employee feels about each individual motivator. We
already know from the team (and it is in Keith's individual Map) report that he
feels 1/10, 9/10, and 1/10 about his top three motivators, and we also know Keith
has a narrow score range. So what do you think the next six numbers reveal about
Keith's motivations at work, if they reveal anything?

Three key things to notice here might be:

1. There is a pattern of low satisfaction, 1/10, across four other motivators,
    suggesting a wider discontent with this organisation and how it operates.
2. Curiously, Keith's lowest motivator, which means his least important, he is
    very satisfied with, at 8/10. This is curious because it is anomalous. How?
    It suggests not that Keith is truly an expert in what he does, but that he
    perceives himself as being very good at what he does; and this would
    accentuate what he also perceives as being his lack of recognition (Star, 1/
    10) for his expertise. The question becomes, then, do we have an indicator
    here that perhaps Keith has a rather inflated view of his own abilities that
    does not correspond with how others see him?
3. Finally, we notice that Keith is not especially motivated by money (Builder) but
    he has scored this only 1/10 in terms of satisfaction rating. Now we could put
    this down to his general malaise and discontent – 6 out of 9 motivators scoring
    1/10! But we need to look more widely afield here. From the organisational
    viewpoint the question of whether their salaries are sufficient to attract and
    retain employees is important. If we go back to Figure 4.1 we see that one other
    person in the team actually has Builder in their top three, Amanda. And we also
    see that of her top three motivators, the Builder is the least satisfactory to her
    (5/10). So this is something we need to explore further.[6]

We have covered Keith's case in some detail and this is very necessary for at
least two powerful reasons. The first is that this is what it takes to really listen
to an employee's voice: we are using a Motivational Map, we are studying
numbers which don't lie, but even so there is still no automatic read-out that
this means *this* or it simply – simplistically – means *that*. If we are going to
understand people – and give them a voice – then the second reason is that we
need to spend some time on them, although not necessarily equal time; it will
depend – how important are they to our organisation, how complex is the
situation, and how subtle are the motivational drives?

Activity 4.7

But, of course, Keith is one person. We have identified just three (Figure 4.3)
from the full team in Figure 4.1. What about the employee voices of John and

Clive? We will not go into the same level of detail here, but we can ask this key question: given their satisfaction scorings, which motivator should the manager of these two employees be addressing as a first priority?

John   Expert   10/10 Spirit   5/10   Director   8/10   86%
Clive   Searcher 1/10   Expert   1/10   Defender   1/10   10%

Unless there is clear evidence to the contrary, the manager would not attempt to address John's top motivator, the Expert, because that is already fully satisfied at 10/10. The weakest link that contributes to his overall high score of 86% is his second motivator, Spirit, which is only 5/10. Thus, giving John more autonomy and freedom would seriously boost his overall levels of energy and motivation. But – and there's always a *but* in Motivational Maps – we need to note in passing two interesting points: one, that like Keith, John feels good about his levels of control, 8/10. So the question might be: is there a pattern emerging? Does giving people control and responsibility indicate a really positive feature of this team, or even possibly for this organisation? And second, like Keith, only with different motivators, John is conflicted, for his desire to be free (Spirit) directly conflicts with his desire for more control (Director)! So here again, given the complexity, we might (in the real world of consultancy delivery) – as we did for Keith – drill down with the advanced 22 numbers.

But moving on, what about Clive? His score of being just 10% motivated is truly 'dreadful'[7] – not something any manager wants to see – and a clear indication of complete disengagement. Clive has been in the organisation a long time, and is competent – but in this state there is clearly no extra-discretionary effort. But which motivator would one focus on, given they are all equally 'distressed' at 1/10? The answer is: the first, the Searcher. For when the satisfaction ratings are equal, then it makes sense to address the motivators in their hierarchical order, since Searcher is obviously more important to Clive. This is doubly so, since unlike Keith, the scoring for Clive's top motivator, 35/40 (Figure 4.7), is so much higher, and so more critically important to him.

Activity 4.8

What three key points about Clive do you pick out from these scores?

There are in fact a lot of 'key' points that we could comment on here. We observe that, like Keith, Clive also has six motivators that he rates only 1/10 satisfaction with! Clearly, many aspects of his work do not inspire him. But here are three interesting points that require further dialogue with Clive, and which might help unpick what needs to happen to help stimulate his motivation:

1.   Clearly, his most important motivator, Searcher – making a difference, being on mission – is not being met at all. Thus, what difference is Clive

Analysis for Clive: Raw Results

Motivator	Score	PMA Score / 10
Searcher	35	1
Expert	30	1
Defender	25	1
Creator	25	1
Director	18	1
Builder	15	7
Friend	13	1
Spirit	10	5
Star	9	5
PMAScore	10%	
ClusterImportance		
Relationship(R)	26%	
Achievement(A)	35%	
Growth(G)	39%	

Figure 4.7 Clive's 22 numbers

making in his work? We need to ensure both more *and* higher quality feedback from his customers.

2. Training and development is also vital to Clive, but again this is only given a 1/10 satisfaction rating. Again, and in discussion with him, there is a high probability that the most obvious solution would be to assign him a coach (whether internally or externally would need to be established) for a 6- or 12-month period.

3. And less obviously, but fascinatingly, how is it that the one motivator that he is relatively happy with, the Builder (7/10), suggests the organisation is paying well, but his third motivator, Defender, or security, is only rated 1/10? Usually, but not always, being paid well makes one feel secure. So what is the issue here?

In the foregoing account of listening to and capturing the employee voice through Motivational Maps, we have, because we have drilled down intensively, got to what we might call a micro-level of detail. We make no apology for this; it is highly necessary, as the above results show,[8] and most texts in our experience discuss macro issues and principles, so the reader is left thinking: yes, I agree with that but how, exactly, do you do it? But that said, there are some important principles relevant to the employee voice that are worth considering.

First, our mind-set and attitudes need to be unequivocally positive, and this is something that organisations have to insist upon at all, and especially at senior, levels. Five things are important here but, before commenting on them, please take one more peek at Figure 4.1. You will remember that we said in the footnote that Sajid in this real-life example was the actual manager of the team. What, then, should we – that is, management – as a minimum requirement be looking for in Sajid's map results?

The answer to this question is that the minimum requirement for a successful team is that Sajid's motivational score should be at the very least be higher than the average for the team. We will say more about this in Chapter 5, but we see now that the team score is 66% and Sajid's is 88%, well above. In fact, Sajid is the most highly motivated team member, which is as it should be since he is the leader. It is impossible to expect high levels of motivation when our leader is less motivated than we are; we take our cues from the leader. What possible reason can there be to be motivated if our leader is less so than ourselves?

And this rationale spills over into the mind-set and attitudes that are crucial to the culture of the organisation that we wish to create and experience. If we do not walk the talk, it cannot happen. So what are the five mind-sets that we need to develop at a high level?

The first, and overarching principle, and the one that is perhaps more important than any other is what is called 'high challenge/high support'.[9] This stems from the concept of high expectations.[10] Expectations are critical and primary because they are our beliefs about the future and its outcomes. At a rudimentary level, if we believe that events will turn out badly for us, then that is what tends to happen; the universe mirrors or reflects, or perhaps more accurately, finally catches up to represent externally what we believe about it internally. Thus, what we believe about our employees is crucial. To take one simple 'belief' that when we reflect on it, shows how dangerous our language has become: do we believe that we employ 'human resources' or do we employ people? And further, do we believe that people want to do a good job and will do one if we support them, or do we believe that all workers are in it for themselves, they need to be tightly controlled, and all 'skiving' must be rigorously repressed?[11]

Our expectations, then, are going to have an inordinate effect on our employees – or, our people!

We can probably see from Figure 4.8 that each quadrant will attract a certain type of manager who will create that sort of 'culture' within their team or immediate sphere of influence. Clearly, only one quadrant is acceptable if we want high achievement: high support and high challenge.

Activity 4.9

How would you describe each of the four types of managers that may inhabit each of the four quadrants? Or put another way, how would you describe a

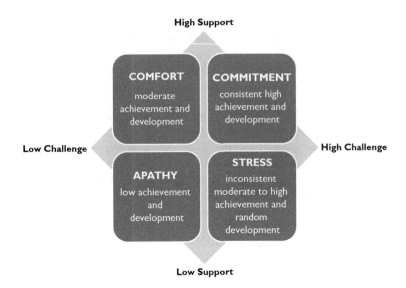

Figure 4.8 High challenge and high support

manager who was 'high support/high challenge', and so on for the other three quadrants? And although our general view is that the best or most consistent place to be is in the 'high challenge/high support' zone, are there any situations you can think of when perhaps another of the quadrants might be useful?

Low challenge/low support is where, effectively, a manager has abdicated responsibility for managing altogether. This person might be termed the Quitter. That said, there may be a very occasional and rare use for it: if one had complete confidence in an employee, or confidence they could tackle the work, task or present situation, then one might leave them to it. But any prolonged use of this style, even deliberately deployed (and let's be frank, it's usually incompetence or indolence that is its source) will lead to profound apathy – disengagement – in all employees affected.

Low challenge/high support is where, effectively, a manager has abdicated responsibility for results but not for people. This person might be termed the Carer. This can be a very 'comfy' situation, what we like to call a 'country club' mentality. Dangerously, of course, it easily leads to groupthink[12] and to no-one ever rocking the boat by challenging either ideas or the state of progress towards a given goal. But, as with the Quitter style, one possible situation where its utilisation might prove handy is when a new employee joins the team. Equally, when an employee is appointed to a new role within an organisation, or someone is having trouble understanding what is expected of them. But if we stay in the Carer quadrant as managers we will end up in comfort, with like-minded and comfortable-to-be-with people, which really is another word for complacency; and complacency invariably leads to underachievement.

Low support/high challenge is where, effectively, a manager has abdicated responsibility for people but not for results. This person might be termed the Driver. Not surprisingly, this style can seem relentless, and is perhaps the one we most associate with 'successful' managers in the UK and the USA. Success, possibly, but always at a price to be paid later in people costs and wastage. But again, there is potentially a point at which the Driver is a good style to adopt, albeit temporarily: when dealing with a very experienced employee, with whom you are very confident, and to whom you wish to delegate extra responsibility. However, this confidence you have needs to be based entirely on their skills and abilities relevant to the job to be done, and not based on what they are currently doing. Clearly, if sustained over a long period the Driver style will lead to stress, because employees being driven this way end up 'running on empty'.

High support/high challenge is where, effectively, a manager has accepted responsibility for people and for results. This person might be termed the Engager. This is where the manager wants to spend their time in seriously both challenging and supporting their employees. This approach is the one most likely to lead to performance and productivity. But we need to be aware even here of the seven-day week principle: no matter how well we perform, we all need one day off a week. In other words, to perform at an optimum level, we need rest, relaxation, change of pace or gear, or just sheer fun and play. So unremitting challenge, even with support, needs to be considered in the long run as potentially deleterious as its effect will be one of frustration: the sense that high performing and highly able people never get to finish anything because the next 'thing' is always underway. Thus, reducing challenge for relevant blocks of time to allow recuperation can be useful.

With these ideas in mind, it would be good for managers, and indeed even individuals faced with big tasks and projects at work, to consider what the challenges are and simultaneously to work out what the support might be, for by now we should be seeing that one without the other is oftentimes disastrous. So, for example, here are three typical and generic challenges (Figure 4.9) that most organisations face at some time or other.

Activity 4.10

What challenges do you have ahead? What support do you need? What support will you supply to others that you are responsible for?

Finally, in this chapter, the other four mind-sets or attitudes are shown in Figure 4.10.

We will be considering these in more detail in Chapter 8.

Challenge	Support
To improve the quality of customer satisfaction	Coaching programme helping employees deliver a higher quality service and gain greater job satisfaction
To increase the productivity and efficiency of teams	Review of roles and responsibilities across teams; training programme on team building for all teams; rewards for performance based on motivational profiles
To reduce employee absenteeism, or staff turnover	Listening to the employee voice; motivational rewards using Motivational Maps

Figure 4.9 Your challenges and support

Figure 4.10 Four key mind-sets for enabling the employee voice

Notes

1 Jacob Morgan, *The Employee Experience Advantage*, John Wiley (2017) remarks, 'Unfortunately, with all the talk of engagement and with all the trainings and rankings of organisations around the world, engagement has remained relatively unchanged despite our collective investments'.
2 For examples, typical questions like, 'My supervisor encourages my career growth' or 'My co-workers are friendly and helpful', can easily become not an opportunity to be honest, but to make a 'point' about someone or others within or without the group.
3 That is to say, 'invisible' emotions and desires, which we may not even know ourselves, become transparent – or visible – through the results of the Maps.
4 Keep in mind that this may be no reflection on the manager, which is Sajid in this real example; it may be that Clive simply does not fit the team and needs to be moved.

5 The rank order of all Maps is correct even when scores are equal; a unique algorithm enables us to rank order them even though they may appear 'equal'. But that said, it does mean of course that the difference in intensity is fractional rather than huge.

6 Simply lack of space prevents us doing this, but working with organisations, and if this were our starting point, then we would want to check other 'advanced' scores, and also check across teams to see whether employees generally rated their remuneration as being less than satisfactory on a consistent basis.

7 We are not being judgemental here: it is dreadful for Clive to be only 10% motivated, never mind the fact that his employer will also experience problems with this employee as a result of this low score. The key issue is not to be judgemental, but to take this as a baseline score from which we can improve the situation.

8 Clive as a result of this process went, within a six-month period, to becoming – unbelievably almost – 100% motivated *and* one of the organisation's top performers across the whole of the UK. The attention paid to him at this level of detail was profound. And, as a sidebar, we have deliberately chosen this team from the hundreds we have, because of the specifically low – and so difficult – motivational scores. People can be turned round with the right approach.

9 The model of high challenge/high support is widely prevalent in education, learning and development scenarios; it originally stems from the work of Lev Vygotsky and his book, *Mind in Society*, Harvard University Press (1978).

10 Without repeating all the information available in the first volume in this series, James Sale, *Mapping Motivation*, Routledge (2016), expectations are critically important to motivation itself: Chapter 2, 'The Roots of Motivation' established that our motivation derives from three primary sources – our personality, our self-concept, and our expectations. Expectations are our beliefs about future outcomes.

11 This question, or a variant of it, was originally posed as part of Douglas McGregor's influential Theory X and Y of the 1960s: *The Human Side of Enterprise*, McGraw-Hill (1960). Theory Y assumed that people, under the right circumstances, learn not only to accept responsibility, but to seek it.

12 Groupthink, a concept outlined by Irving Janis, *Victims of Goupthink: A Psychological Study of Foreign-Policy Decisions and Fiascos*, Houghton, Mifflin (1972).

Chapter 5

Engaging managers, motivation, skills and recruitment

We said earlier that the MacLeod Report refers to four enablers that underpin effective engagement, and that they were all not only vital but interdependent. But we averred too that if only one of them could be fulfilled, then 'engaging managers' was the single most important enabler.[1] This is perhaps controversial; a perfectly good case could be made for saying that the strategic narrative is the most important component, for it drives the other three. And, actually, this is true: the narrative is the compelling logic – the *why*? – that drives employers in the first place, and employees subsequently, to want to engage in motivational and productive behaviours. But let's be clear here: the narrative is just that – it's a story, a communication device, words that staff in the past have been all too familiar with. We talk the talk, but we don't walk it. That is why we claim that the single most important enabler of engagement delivery is going to be 'engaging managers',[2] for any organisation may – without reference to engagement methodologies and theories – find itself with a highly productive and engaged workforce simply because they have spent some time and effort recruiting top-class managers to positions of importance, and – voila! – watch what happens.

So let's unpack this phrase, 'engaging manager', a little before exploring more how we can achieve this. First, the expression itself can be slightly confusing. Indeed, when we say 'engaging managers' do we mean that we are engaging them? That is, recruiting them? No, although of course we do want to do that. What we mean is that the managers have the ability to 'engage' their staff. Thus, as the MacLeod Report puts it:

> Engaging Managers are at the heart of this organisational culture – they facilitate and empower rather than control or restrict their staff; they treat their staff with appreciation and respect and show commitment to developing, increasing and rewarding the capabilities of those they manage.
>
> MacLeod (2009)[3]

Further, they cite research that indicates that 80% of the variations in staff engagement stems from the line manager. People 'join organisations but leave managers'. This is, again, a vital point to understand: on the ground, away from all theories and board rooms, the managers are impacting everything, for good or ill.

So, the role and performance of the manager is key. We have already outlined in Chapter 3 the elements of what constitutes performance; how might this apply, then, to developing engaging managers? However, before we come to the primary issues of skills and motivation, there is another concern that MacLeod and other experts in the field frequently refer to; indeed, we have ourselves referred to it above when we talk of not walking the talk. This is the principle of consistency; as MacLeod says, 'We need consistencies between values and behaviours'. Gary Hamel[4] gets to the root of the difficulty of this when he comments: 'In my experience, most managers support the *idea* of empower-ment, but become noticeably less enthusiastic when confronted with the neces-sary corollary – to enfranchise employees you must disenfranchise managers'.[5]

Activity 1

Given this issue, what actions might senior management undertake to counter the inertial 'drag' of not wanting to give up power and control? Make a list of what you think is appropriate and helpful.

There is no prescriptive list of activities that will definitively counter the inertia of the status quo,[6] but Figure 5.1 shows some things that we think definitely need addressing as part of an engagement strategy.

The importance of values[7] cannot be overestimated, as well as understanding the difference between explicit values and implicit.[8]

The consequences of these six areas for review (Figure 5.2) are profound when we consider them in respect of the engaging manager, and they are profound too when we consider how Mapping Motivation is relevant to all six areas.

The Organisational Motivational Map[9] is important not only in engagement, but in change and leadership programmes. Game playing[10] is a psychopathol-ogy, which is the opposite of being engaged, although those practising it may well attempt to *appear* engaged.

As we progress through this book we will see an expansion of some of these ideas. But for now, to return to MacLeod, what are the key requirements of managers in order to make then engaging? MacLeod reckons from their distilla-tion of all the submissions they received that there are three.

Activity 5.2

MacLeod defined the requirements as 'behaviours'. What do you think are the top three behaviours that engaging managers need to be effective? Reflect on good managers that you have known. What were the key things they did? Make a list of three things.

Figure 5.3 shows the three required behaviours according to MacLeod.

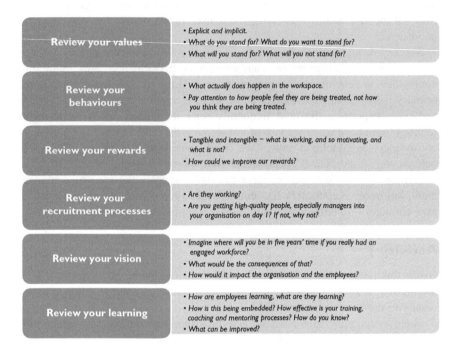

Figure 5.1 Seeking to overcome inertia and the status quo

So managers need to be clear about expectations, and they need to be continually coaching; they need interpersonal skills and empathy, and they need to bring efficient order to what is going on – namely, the work flow. These are largely great behaviours, but we would like to expand these into distinct skill sets, talk about these skills sets, and then relate this to how we produce engaging managers. What, then, are the core skills underpinning the kinds of behaviours that MacLeod advocates?

Activity 5.3

We have established what the behaviours are, but what do you think are the top four *skills* that would enable an engaging manager to fulfil those behaviours?

According to Rob Goffee and John Hunt,[11] there are four key skills that underpin what they call the 'high performing manager', which we consider synonymous with the engaging manager. These four skill sets are shown in Figure 5.4.

Activity 5.4

Look at Figure 5.5. If you are a manager then rank yourself out of 10 (10 is high, you fully possess this skill; 1 is low, you completely lack this skill). Be

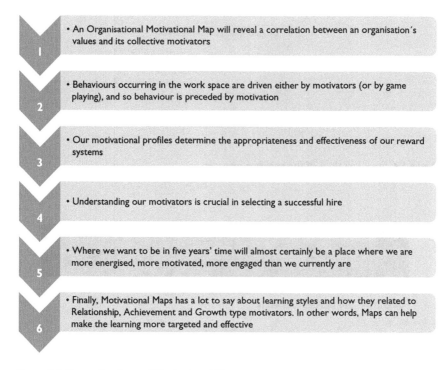

Figure 5.2 Six applications of Motivational Maps

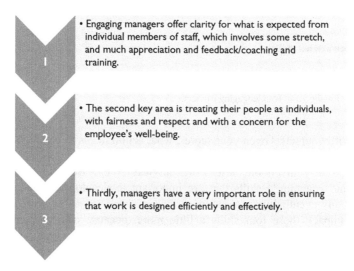

Figure 5.3 MacLeod's three behaviours of engaging managers

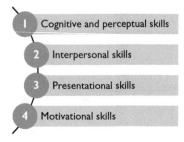

1 Cognitive and perceptual skills

2 Interpersonal skills

3 Presentational skills

4 Motivational skills

Figure 5.4 Four key skills of the engaging manager

Key Engaging Manager Skill	Score/10	Action to be Taken
Cognitive and perceptual skills		
Interpersonal skills		
Presentational skills		
Motivational skills		

Figure 5.5 Rating your four engaging manager skills

honest with yourself. Given your scores, what action needs to be taken? Keep in mind that if any score is 6, then that is average only. Even if you are not a manager, rate yourself on these scores anyway. Why? Because they all both people and coaching[12] skills that are important to develop and understand in virtually any eventuality or situation.

Let's unpack these four skills a little more, because clarity is vital. First, cognitive and perceptual skills is really a posh way of saying: *thinking –* thinking skills! They are rarer than one might suppose since many people like to work (and play for that matter) on automatic pilot, or to allow custom or habit to dictate what is to be done.[13] But one thing Goffee specifically identifies as critical in the engaging manager's armoury is the ability to reduce chunks of information to simple and understandable frameworks. In other words, to control and manipulate complexities so that they are truly manageable. This is exactly MacLeod's point about the 'very important role in ensuring that work is designed efficiently and effectively'. The thinking skill we want to inculcate actually relates to 80/20 or Pareto[14] thinking: how do we lessen waste (of resources),[15] which is efficiency, and how do we leverage greater results from the resources we have, which is effectiveness? Notice the difficulty of the mind-set we are promoting here: reducing waste requires one kind of thinking that is very detail-orientated, enabling us to see where wastage occurs; enhancing results – and so growing – requires a very different kind of thinking, one which is expansive and perhaps more 'blue-sky' in that we have to imagine what is not yet possible.

This latter point relates to the oft-made distinction between leaders and managers. That the former 'do the right things' – which is effective – whilst the latter 'do things right' – which is efficient. It would appear that the engaging manager is expected to do both – a big ask, then! We need to keep in mind the potential contradiction here, and to be clear that if we cannot have perfection – both efficacy and efficiency – on what side do we need to err for the managers we require in our organisation? Our answers will depend on at least three things: the type of work to be done, the sector we are operating within, and the stage of growth of the organisation at that moment.

Interpersonal skills are the second skill we need to focus on. Goffee brings in an important idea here that is absent from MacLeod's three behaviours: interpersonal skills are about developing people *and* building teams. Clearly, when we give staff 'some stretch, and much appreciation and feedback/ coaching and training', we are developing people. Equally, treating them as 'individuals' along with fairness and respect also are extremely positive. But notice here how all the skills are directed at the individual, yet a primary skill that the engaging manager must have is the ability to build strong teams. This idea is really an extension of the first skill, which is thinking through how we become more effective; for after all, what is team building but the ability to leverage individuals so that the product of their output is greater than the sum of their parts? It is to create a synergy between people through which a tremendous productivity is unleashed via collaboration. In our book *Mapping Motivation*[16] we talk of groups[17] versus teams. Groups achieve an arithmetic level of productivity, whereas teams produce a geo-metric level. That's a huge difference over time, although, of course, initially productivity seems to lag in teams as one has to build them consciously, whilst allowing individuals in a group to operate just on their own targets takes little time at all.

Third are presentational skills. What does Goffee mean by these? These skills come down to presentation and communication abilities. So it's not just what we say, it's how we say it; it's not just content, it's process also. And we might add that just as skill number two had an echo in skill number one, so skill number three has just such an echo in skill number two. For surely, when we skilfully present and communicate we are, in fact, engaging in advanced interpersonal skills? One distinction might be, however, that the focus specifically on presentation and communication abilities is more about the ability of the engaging manager to influence and persuade, effectively, their employees. Of course, overtly or not, almost all people, especially employees, are desperate to be led. Why? Because being well led means reducing uncertainty, and thereby insecurity. Therefore, presenting and communicating take on a particular significance; for the failure to present and communicate – what we are doing, why we are doing it, and how we are going to go about doing it – is to present and communicate very badly indeed. In such situations staff do not know what to think or believe, and so rumour, misunderstandings, distortion, and resentment gain the upper hand. And this returns us to skill number two – for not to present to one's employees is also a form of disrespect, and is fundamentally unfair: how can we expect people to perform if they don't know the what, why and how? So, interestingly, Goffee talks about the importance of the engaging manager spending some 80% of their time interfacing with employees. 'Presenting', then, is not about some being some TV-style evangelist, or some hyper-active motivational speaker who loves addressing the followers at huge rallies, but it is about being there, walking the talk, explaining, encouraging, supporting, and communicating what it is we are trying to achieve and why it is important.

We see how the three skills so far – and the fourth is no different – are not really three or four things, but one package. We need the engaging manager to have *the complete works*! And this completeness involves skill sets that are interlocking and related. So our fourth skill is, unsurprisingly, supportive of both our second (interpersonal) and third (presentational) skills, since when we interact with another human being in the workplace it is usually better to be motivational than not, and the same is true when we communicate or present, and thus wish to influence others.

So, finally, the fourth skill is motivational. I suppose this must be our favourite, given the title of our book, but what does Goffee mean by it (writing before Motivational Maps were available)? He means being motivational by creating stretching goals and by being results orientated. This is good, so far as it goes, but it is old school and does not take account of the fact that people are motivationally different, and this means that even whilst ambitious goal-setting[18] and results orientation seem 'motivational', actually, for some people – some employees – they are not. There, we've said it: goals and results don't motivate everybody! Goal-setting and results, for all the worldwide focus on them in the personal development movement and corporate commercial programmes, do appeal to the 'Achievement' type motivators, that is the Director, Builder and Expert, especially, and to some degree at the fringe ends of these motivators, the Star and the Creator, but they are less important to the other four motivators, the Defender, the Friend, the Spirit and the Searcher (see Figure 5.6); or perhaps more accurately, they are significant only as a by-product of these four motivators' other and more primary concerns. Keep in mind, too, that we may have an engaging manager who does not herself have the classic 'Achievement' type motivators in her profile.[19] So the way forward may be direct – because goals and results do motivate – or indirect: we structure work and reward the individual on the basis of what they really want, whilst not losing sight of the goals and results we are trying to achieve.[20] How do we do this? By using Motivational Maps!

Where do we go from here then? It seems a number of points are crystal clear. That we need in the first instance a recruitment process that selects people who either already are 'engaging managers' or who have the potential to be so. This is important in that we don't wish to have the ongoing problem of 'square pegs in round holes': appointing staff who are going to be forever incapable of rising to the challenge of achieving 'engaging manager' performance levels.

Second, we need to ensure that consistency of approach and walking the talk is endemic to an organisation, and that everyone from the top to the bottom is called to account. This can only happen when a specific and tailored value system is made explicit and mandatory. There can be no compromise

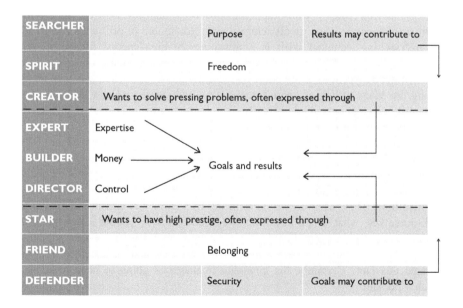

Figure 5.6 Motivators primarily for goals and results

with values, any more than there can be with integrity; we either have values or we don't. There is no middle way with this. We may have a vision that circumstances or commercial factors necessitate we change; that's sometimes how business works. But our values have to be sacrosanct, and this point cannot be emphasised enough, for it is easy in the competitive heat of organisational battles to lose sight of this fact, and to cut corners. Doing so ultimately signals the demise of the organisation, as Enron[21] and many others have discovered.

Third, we have to equip and support managers at all levels. This includes particularly ensuring the four skills sets we have outlined are present, but alongside this the attitudes that are critical. For example, some line managers are confident and competent to work with survey data and develop action plans accordingly; others may not be. Understandably, negative data can be met with defensiveness and managers can feel confused about where to go for support in developing their action plan. Thus, organisations need to address these kind of issues. How do we do this?

And fourth, we need reward strategies in place that genuinely motivate employees, and not a one-size-fits-all approach, which sadly is all too common. Here, too, Motivational Maps has something important to contribute.

Let's look, then, at these four issues one by one, and give some practical ways in which we can improve what we do organisationally in all of them. First, recruitment of the engaging manager. The issue here is how do Motivational Maps help us get the right or the superior candidate?

Before we say anything else we need to keep in mind that motivation is energy; as Lou Adler,[22] with others, has observed, high levels of energy are the 'universal success factor' in all achievement. No amount of brilliant strategizing or overarching technical skills is a substitute for high energy. Indeed, as has often been observed, sheer hard work can get us through most problems, and to do that work we need motivation and commitment. So, when we talk about using the Maps to help in recruitment we are talking about them helping us to establish whether a candidate really is a high-energy individual – or simply someone who seems to be one at interview!

Usually, the Motivational Map recruitment process has five stages (Figure 5.7).

We are not going to go through every aspect of these five stages here, but to focus on one thing that is especially useful; namely, given that each short-listed candidate – that is to say, the cream of the long-list crop – has done a Motivational Map, what do we do with it? To answer this question we have to ask ourselves: what is the key thing we need to know[23] about a candidate in order to want to appoint them? What we need to know is: is this person a genuinely high-energy person who has consistently and persistently demonstrated this fact? Certainly, the engaging m.anager is going to need to be just such a person!

Typically, to establish whether this is the case the interviewer asks a question such as:

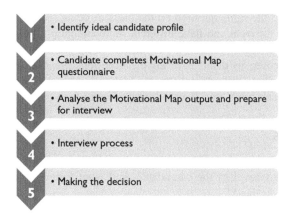

1 • Identify ideal candidate profile

2 • Candidate completes Motivational Map questionnaire

3 • Analyse the Motivational Map output and prepare for interview

4 • Interview process

5 • Making the decision

Figure 5.7 Five stage recruitment process using Motivational Maps

> Please tell me, what in your current position has been your most significant achievement?

Or this could be phrased as:

> Please tell me, what are you most proud of in your work at ABC over the last year or so?

Or even:

> How have you shown initiative in your present position?

These, or variants of them, are great questions, because they get a 'first take' on what should be a high-energy performance – 'significant' or 'proud of' or 'initiative'. If they can't answer that question, where can we go with them? And if they can, then we need to drill down further to establish exactly what their part, their contribution, their role is or was in the achievement. To do this, then, we ask for more specifics such as: the nature of the problem solved, duration and dates, bottom line impact, challenges involved and implementation steps, the candidate's actual role in delivery, and so on. We question deeply rather than widely.

Now this is a great process, but using Motivational Maps at this point adds massively in two important ways: first, it can make the 'high energy' question far more targeted and specific; second, it also confirms the consistency (or not) of the candidate's energy – and values – with what they are doing. It becomes a sort of check on the issue of consistency that we mentioned earlier as being critical. How does it do this? The answer to this question also reveals another benefit: by not asking everyone the same question on the basis of being 'equal', but by realising that people are different and have different motivational profiles, the interviewer can ask 'fair' questions based on the candidates' Map profiles.

We cannot cover in detail here all the questions we use, because that too involves a detailed 'drill down', but to kick off with the 'root' and 'check' questions for each motivator, have a look at Figure 5.8.

Activity 5.5

Why are these Root and check questions important? How do they gain access to the actual energy level of the candidate? And what follow-up questions might you use based on these?

Notice a number of things here about this process (we will use the Searcher as our example). Firstly, we do not say 'Looking through your Motivational Map, I see that making a difference is important to you …' Why is that? Because we wish to stress that this appointment does not depend on the Map profile. On the contrary, if – big IF – a candidate we are considering (who has been short-listed, has done a Map, and Searcher is their number one motivator), has a 'valid' CV, then surely it will automatically tell us that making a difference is inherent in everything that candidate has been doing. Think about it: why would it not? Their Map reveals they want to make a difference – whether they consciously are aware of it or not – so their 'want' should have translated into action at the work level; the source of this information, the Maps, is entirely incidental. Keep it out of the discussion, then: focus on what is important – whether the candidate really is a person who makes a difference!

Second, the root question is a why question. This, then, is attempting to see just how self-aware the candidate is about their motives and why they do what they do. Clearly, this is important when considering employing an engaging manager, for a lack of self-awareness, especially of one's own motivations and emotional clarity, hardly bodes well for their ability to read other people's, and reading other people's is core to what the engaging manager does. So the answer to this question – or any of its eight variants for the other eight motivators – is fascinating and revealing.

Thirdly, we reach the check question. This is, of course, our variation on the classic recruiter's question: *Please tell me, what in your current position has been your most significant achievement?* But now it is more targeted: we are aligning the answer not just to some big organisational achievement that we all think grand, but to something done that has an emotional alignment with the person. Thus, this is subtler, gentler, more deceptive in its quiet way; indeed, almost casual. We – the organisation – have just agreed with you that making a difference is critical to you, the candidate, and in the root question you have told us why. Given that, now tell us about how you think you have made that difference.

MOTIVATOR	ROOT QUESTION: Looking through your application, I see that	CHECK QUESTION: I see that
SEARCHER	Making a difference is important to you. Can you tell me why that is so?	Making a difference is important to you. Tell me how you've made a difference in your current role?
SPIRIT	Being able to make your own decisions is important to you. Can you tell me why that is so?	Being able to make your own decisions is important to you. Tell me about when you've been able to make your own decisions in your current role? What happened?
CREATOR	Being able to innovate is important to you. Can you tell me why that is so?	Being able to innovate is important to you. Tell me about when you've been able to innovate in your current role? What happened?
EXPERT	Demonstrating expertise is important to you. Can you tell me why that is so?	Demonstrating expertise is important to you. Tell me about when you've been able to demonstrate expertise in your current role? What happened?
BUILDER	Money is important to you. At the risk of sounding obvious, can you tell me why that is so?	Money is important to you. Tell me about when you've been able to make more money in your current role? What happened/how did you do it?
DIRECTOR	Actively managing is important to you. At the risk of sounding obvious, can you tell me why this is so?	Actively managing is important to you. Tell me about when you've been able to actively manage in your current role? What happened?
STAR	Receiving recognition is important to you. At the risk of sounding obvious, can you tell me why this is so?	Receiving recognition is important to you. Tell me about when you've been receiving recognition in your current role? What happened?
FRIEND	Being part of a team is important to you. At the risk of sounding obvious, can you tell me why this is so?	Being part of a team is important to you. Tell me about when you've been part of a team in your current role? What happened?
DEFENDER	Security is important to you. At the risk of sounding obvious, can you tell me why this is so?	Security is important to you. Tell me about when you've felt secure in your current role? What happened? How did that come about?

Figure 5.8 Root and check motivational questions for recruitment

Activity 5.6

The principle of what we are saying is true for all nine motivators, but can you feel how much more difficult it is to answer our check question compared with the standard recruitment question? Keep in mind, the question appears easier! And why is that? Make a note of your answers to these two questions.

To answer the standard recruitment question is actually easy (although of course weak candidates will invent, fabricate and generally exaggerate their achievements) because we all know what organisations want to hear: namely, that we increased revenue, or satisfied the customer, or built a strong team, or impacted the bottom-line and so on. And that is fine so far as it goes because we do want these things. But to ask – in the case of the Searcher motivator – how you have 'made a difference' is another order of answer. We can see this clearly if we simply interrogate the traditional answers above: so, if someone were to say, 'I increased revenues by 19%'. Yes, but – what difference did that make? 'I created a strong team'. Yes, but what difference did that make? Here the interviewer is 'engaging' the candidate on their own motivational terms and looking for a deeper level of answer that the more traditional approach often fails to elicit.

And from this check question, the creative question now emerges.[24]

Activity 5.7

What do you think the creative question for the Searcher might now be that would really show which candidates were capable of what?

This is disarmingly simple, isn't it?

And tell me how you think you can make a difference in the post we have open?

Surely, here, the word 'difference' is what we really want to know about this applicant's capability? As we look at the various answers to these three sets of questions alone from the short-listed candidates we will be in a strong and informed position to make a good decision.[25] Keep in mind, no decision can be perfect or always right, but we begin to seriously weight the odds in our favour. Interviewing candidates, it has been said, is like tossing a coin: there is only a 50–50 chance of getting the right person. Using this technology, the odds are more like 70–30 or 80–20 in our experience.

The full list of Creative questions is shown in Figure 5.9.

One important point to re-stress about these questions is that we are not treating the candidates 'equally'; we are treating them fairly. The particular question we will select is based on their motivational profile, and therefore is directly addressing what should be their 'strength'. After all, what motivates tends to be what we practise, and what we practise we tend to get good at. In this way we are actually allowing each candidate to shine[26] with their own special motivational energies, as they are reflected in their work behaviours.

SEARCHER	And tell me how you think you can make a difference in the post we have open?
SPIRIT	And tell me how you think you will be able to make your decisions in the post we have open? What are your expectations?
CREATOR	And tell me how you think you will be able to innovate in the post we have open? What are your expectations?
EXPERT	And tell me how you think you will be able to demonstrate expertise in the post we have open? What are your expectations?
BUILDER	And tell me how you think you will be able to earn more in the post we have open? What are your expectations?
DIRECTOR	And tell me how you think you will be able to actively manage in the post we have open? What are your expectations?
STAR	And tell me how you think you will be receiving recognition of the kind you want in the post we have open? What are your expectations?
FRIEND	And tell me how you think you will be part of a team in the post we have open? What are your expectations?
DEFENDER	And tell me how you think your need for security will be met in the post we have open? What are your expectations?

Figure 5.9 Nine creative map recruitment questions

Activity 5.8

Consider your own Motivational Map profile, especially your top motivator. Which motivator is it? Ask yourself the creative question and make a note of your answer. And particularly note the second part of the question: *what are your expectations?* If we think about this from the candidate's perspective we can surely see that thinking this through may help weed out applications, or accepting jobs, from organisations that will never be 'right' for you.

Given that there are nine motivators, then there are going to be nine sets of questions around each motivator. These questions are going to probe the why, the what and the how of the motivator.[27] Because the motivator reflects the energy of the candidate, then we are 'tuning' into the very aspect of their psyche that should be productive. Drill down may still be necessary after these sets of questions, but in themselves they directly get to the core of the individual's energy and help them to be able to express it – if, indeed, they have it.

Activity 5.9

Now review your own Map profile. What is your number one motivator? Identify it and then use it to answer for yourself the three relevant questions (root, check and creative) for your motivator. Thus, you will be considering:

why it is important to you; what you experienced of it in your current role; and how you might experience it in your future work.

If we just take the first motivator, the Searcher, then what are we looking for? Well, here is what we are NOT looking for:

Question 1: *Looking through your application, I see that making a difference is important to you. Can you tell me why that is so?*
Ineffective answers might be:

> *No, not really.*
> *I just like to.*
> *Who said that?*

An effective answer might be:

> Yes, perhaps the best thing would be for me to tell you about what I am currently doing, and most pleased about. I have spent the last six months managing Project Team A and our mission has been to write some quite complex software code to solve a big problem that our client has. This is to do with our client's online payment system, which currently isn't working well, and they are losing clients and so money as a result. The great thing is – when we got our beta-version up, the client could immediately see the difference that this was going to make. I felt so good when their technical director mentioned how well I had held the team together and kept them on target, which had made big difference to their bottom line: this was a game-changer for them, and she said so. That's what I love.

This answer, of course, makes question two redundant, unless we want to ask for another example (so drill down) of when this sort of experience has happened.

Question 2: I see that making a difference is important to you. Tell me how you've made a difference in your current/most recent/last role/job? *Questioned answered for question 1.*

Question 3: *And tell me how you think you can make a difference in the post we have open?*
Ineffective answers might be:

> *Not sure.*
> *I like the salary but am not clear what's involved.*
> *I am very good at maths.*

An effective answer might be:

> Please correct me if I am wrong, but as I understand the role, and what ABC Ltd are looking for, then I believe that I have just the right skills and enthusiasm to make a big difference here. I went on your website and did

some fact-finding on where you currently are with your contract with Big Client Ltd. So I feel that I can easily fit into your team culture, inspire others to give their best, am completely fluent with agile methodology, and as a can-do kind of person I look for great outcomes. So yes, the difference I am going to make is in bringing high energy, expertise, leadership and direction to your team, and this is going to affect your results in a big way.

Clearly, this is all example material, but hopefully the principles of what we talking about are there to see. To get the right person – the truly engaging manager – we need to drill down on their motivators and see what their energy levels are really like.

In the next chapter we are going to consider the other three issues for having engaging managers: values and consistency, the four skills, and reward strategies.

Notes

1 'The role of the manager is also key to the engagement levers with the greatest impact on discretionary effort identified by CLC research on this topic: understanding how to do one's job, a belief in the importance of it and understanding how to complete one's work. These are more critical in driving effort than any other day-to-day work factors including resources, job quality, suitability for role and personal goals'. The MacLeod Report, David MacLeod et al., *Engaging for Success: Enhancing Performance through Employee Engagement*, Office of Public Sector Information (2009).
2 'The number one predictor of job satisfaction is the relationship with the manager'. Karin Hurt, CEO of Let's Grow Leaders, Fixing Employee Engagement, Recognition and Engagement essentials presented by HR.com, December 2014.
3 MacLeod Report, op. cit.
4 Gary Hamel, *The Future of Management*, Harvard Business School Press (2007).
5 And as Gary Hamel, op. cit., further observes: 'the redistribution of power is one of the primary means of making organisations more adaptable, more innovative, and more highly engaging'. Clearly, managers are reluctant to give up power and control for all sorts of reasons, including their sense of becoming vulnerable, redundant, and because they didn't go into management in order to abdicate responsibility, as they understand it. This will be particularly acute where the manager has a Director motivator in their top three motivators.
6 'Good ideas and solid concepts have a great deal of difficulty in being understood by those who earn their living by doing it some other way' – Philip Crosby, *Let's Talk Quality*, McGraw-Hill (1989).
7 Arguably, the single most important thing management can do (establishing and communicating values), and also the thing management is least likely to do as it seems so abstract and remote from everyday operations and marketing; but to think so is a huge mistake.
8 The explicit values are what we have on our organisational literature, but the implicit is revealed by what we actually do – so again we come up against this idea of consistency and coherence: are we acting in the way that we explicitly say we believe in? For example, if we say in our literature that we treat people equally but actually pay women less than men for the same role and job (there being no

performance issue relevant to pay here, as performance invariably leads to pay inequality since performances are rarely equal), then our values are inconsistent. The net effect of this over time is demotivation, disengagement and high staff turnover.

9   For more on this application, see our forthcoming book, James Sale, *Mapping Motivation for Strategy and Change*, Routledge (2020).

10   Game playing in Transactional Analysis is where, psychologically, we think 'I lose/ you lose' – creating lose–lose situations rather than win–win. It is always a result of low-esteem, low self-confidence and low self-efficacy. Such people, have a motivational profile which they will claim represents what they really want, but this in fact proves not to be the case: playing their 'game' is more important to them than having satisfying motivators; indeed, the game has become the motivator. It is at the recruitment stage that it is best to weed out such candidates for posts within our organisation. For more on Transactional Analysis see Thomas A. Harris, *I'm OK, You're OK*, Harper and Row (1969).

11   Rob Goffee and John Hunt, The end of management? Classroom versus the boardroom, in Bickerstaffe G. ed., *Mastering Management*, Financial Times/Pitman (1997).

12   For a fuller account of coaching and developing coaching skills, see James Sale and Bevis Moynan, *Mapping Motivation for Coaching*, Routledge (2018).

13   Hence the well-known antidote to this in 'quality' circles where the buzz is for 'continuous improvement'; for this to occur managers (and employees) have to 'think' about their work.

14   For a detailed account of how this works, see our book, James Sale and Bevis Moynan, *Mapping Motivation for Coaching*, Routledge (2018), Chapter 3.

15   There are nine critical resources: money, time, equipment, people skills, knowledge, right attitude, information, space/environment, and agreed co-operation, which can all be 'wasted'. See Chapter 8, Figure 8.11. Also, James Sale, *Mapping Motivation*, Routledge (2016) for more information on these.

16   James Sale, *Mapping Motivation*, Routledge (2016).

17   The distinction between a group and a team is simply that a group is a collection of individuals who happen to be working in a department or faculty (or even something called a 'team') but which do not. By contrast, real teams do these four things. a. share a remit, b. practise interdependency, c. believe in the power of teams, and d. remain accountable. For more, see James Sale, op.cit.

18   One recalls BHAGs – Big Hairy Audacious Goals, an idea explored in Jim Collins, *Good to Great*, Random House (2001).

19   Also keep in mind that usually an individual's profile has three motivators that really 'count' in terms of what they want, so the fact that an Achievement motivator is not their top motivator does not necessarily mean goals and results are not crucial for their well-being.

20   A distinction here, too, that is useful to point out is that whilst Friend and Spirit seem the least motivated by goals and results, we need to keep in mind that when we talk of 'goals and results' in organisational or business terms we are invariably talking of 'content' – that is, profit, sales and other tangibles. But, of course, if we consider a goal to be about a 'process' – how we treat people, for example, or how we manage them and allow autonomy – then the Friend and Spirit are more likely to directly buy-in!

21   When it went bankrupt on 2 December, 2001, Enron employed some 20,000 staff, was a major world electricity, natural gas, and communications supplier, had supposed revenues of nearly $101 billion during 2000 and *Fortune* magazine had named Enron 'America's Most Innovative Company' for six consecutive years! What could go wrong?

22   Lou Adler, *Hire with Your Head: A Rational Way to Make a Gut Reaction* (1998).

23 It is important to stress at this point that one would never make an appointment solely on the basis of a Motivational Map reading, or even the response to a key 'Map' question at interview; one needs to take a holistic view of a candidate and their application.

24 There are in Motivational Maps 'drill-down' questions based on the motivators, and at five levels of questioning: root, check, creative, block and lowest motivator questions. We have in this chapter only considered three of these for purposes of space; the whole issue of recruitment is worthy of a separate book, but block questions involve investigating what happens if the motivator is not being met. So, for the Searcher, this might sound like this:

> Have you ever done work where you received very little or no feedback on how you were doing from anyone? If NO – probe. Really? Never? Ask YOURSELF: Is this a credible answer? If YES – follow up: What did you do? How would you respond if you were working here and didn't receive the kind of feedback you initially envisaged?

And the lowest motivator question is about probing if a motivator that is considered important for a particular role appears as lowest in the candidate's profile. So this question may, for the Searcher as lowest, sound like:

> Is making a difference important to you? If NO – probe. If you were appointed to this role, what differences would you be making over the next three, six, and twelve months? If YES – Tell me how you have made a difference in your current role.

This is very tricky to answer as a question because we already know that the Searcher is lowest here.

25 Depending on circumstances and context, candidates may or may not be given access to their Map result before the interview itself.

26 Keep in mind here: Maps must never be used as the sole determinant of whether somebody is appointed or not; they are a tool to enable a more relevant conversation between applicant and employer to occur; context is everything regarding the use of Maps.

27 The questions given are the starting point. The full drill down is available from Motivational Maps.

Chapter 6

Engaging managers, values, 360-motivational feedback, rewards

In Chapter 5 we investigated MacLeod's views on the engaging manager, and agreed that such managers are essential – indeed, primary – to the establishment of an engaged workforce. But we have developed MacLeod's concepts further, adding ideas from leading management thinkers, and applying Motivational Mapping technology to enable us to realise the 'dream' – or the 'Holy Grail' as it were – of engagement. We have learnt that four factors are critical, and we shared some of our ideas on the first factor, recruitment, at the end of the chapter. In this chapter we are going to cover the other three areas: values and consistency, four key engaging skills, and motivational reward strategies, and we show where Mapping Motivation is particularly useful in achieving all this.

First, then, values and consistency. We have already commented on how indispensable and non-negotiable core and explicit values are. Actually, this is as true in personal life as it is in business or organisational activity at any level. To get to the root of what we are getting at here, Simon Sinek[1] is very helpful, for he writes: 'For values or guiding principles to be truly effective they have to be verbs'.

Activity 6.1

What is the difference between a noun and a verb? Why is a verb a more powerful language with which to express values? Review your personal values – or your organisation's: how are they expressed, as nouns or verbs? If as nouns, what would they be as verbs? How would you re-frame them?

If we go back to school, we remember that nouns are 'things' and that verbs are 'doing words'. We don't need to get more complicated than that to understand that nouns – as things – are passive; and verbs – as doing words – are active. Indeed, verbs are the action words in sentences. Verbs beckon us to do 'stuff'; verb are what change is all about – they are transmitters of change. Thus, to think of values as nouns is to help engender passivity, static thinking and redundant checklists. As Bob Garratt[2] observed, 'A value is a belief in action', and so we need to express it in action terms.

Imagine you work for a typical organisation and you have seen their typical values. What will they look like? Like a list of nouns (see Figure 6.1)!

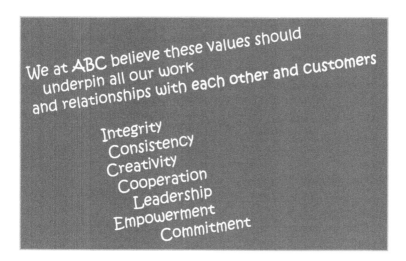

Figure 6.1 Values as nouns list

The seven noun values we have listed are not from any one organisation we have worked with, but they are a random selection of those that we find most often seem to occur. What would they look like expressed as verbs? First, be clear there may be no one word to word correspondence for at least two reasons. First, some nouns don't have convenient verbal forms. Take integrity as a noun: what would be its verb form one-word equivalent? There isn't one. On the other hand, take co-operation and clearly we have the verb to co-operate. However, even should a one-word alternative present itself, we need to stop and think. Actually, what are the behaviours that we want our employees to engage with and in? Simply to insert 'to co-operate' or even 'co-operate' in place of co-operation seems flat. What are the action verbs that manifest themselves when co-operation is occurring?

There cannot be one right answer to this, but, for example, we might suggest: 'To help others achieve their targets', or 'we help each other and customers achieve their goals', or 'we individually do all we can to work together as a team', and so on.

Activity 6.2

We have taken 'co-operation' and spun its value incarnation through three spins! However, each organisation or person can improve on our versions, because they can tailor 'co-operate' to suit their circumstances, needs and situation. Ask the question: what does 'co-operate' mean in our situation? So now consider the other six nouns: convert them into verbs.[3]

Every organisation will need to establish their values for themselves; and although it's useful to check out best practice, it is invariably fatal to just import another organisation's ideas. Values need to emerge from within an organisation and its culture; it needs careful consideration because it has profound ramifications not only in the realm of engagement, but in every other area too. For example, Sinek cites Apple, and shows how its choice of values even drills down to the level of the pop singer[4]/group they choose to front one of their video adverts. There has to be consistency across the whole spectrum of organisational activities; or, put another way, all the actions of an organisation and its employees need to be aligned with their core values.

Mapping Motivation comes in at this point because, as we like to say, motivators aggregated become strong indicators of the actual values lived, as opposed to espoused. What does this mean? It means that at the end of the day whatever the organisation says its values are, its employees have to live these values, and whether they will or not mightily depends on their motivational profile. To see what we mean by this, study Figure 6.2.

Clearly, we are using the traditional 'nouns' here in order to create a short-hand for the ideas we are exploring, but each one of these can be turned into a verb phrase or clause. And we see already some of the key value 'nouns' that we encounter so often in organisations: the values of creativity, leadership, consistency, and so on.

Activity 6.3

Take the first word in the list of possible and wider values and convert the noun into a verbal equivalent. That is, take the nine words, 'fairness, freedom, creativity ... standards' and express what we mean by that as an action within an organisation.[5]

Motivator	Possible and Wider Values
SEARCHER	fairness? tolerance? equality? goodness?
SPIRIT	freedom? democracy? directness? autonomy? liberty?
CREATOR	creativity? openness? curiosity? innovation? beauty?
EXPERT	rationality? truth? honesty? knowledge?
BUILDER	competition? challenge? materialism? results?
DIRECTOR	authority? obedience? discipline? power? leadership?
STAR	respect? sociability? hierarchy? fame?
FRIEND	friendship? love? support? consensus? reciprocity? acceptance?
DEFENDER	standards? consistency? clarity? order?

Figure 6.2 Possible values for the nine motivators

Now, so what? We have laboured this point a bit, but we think it is really crucial to understand, and by so doing understand how Mapping Motivation helps. For imagine the following scenario: your organisation has 'creativity' as one of its top three values. Indeed, you pride yourself on innovative solutions that you can provide your clients or customers, which are much more innovative than your nearest competitor, who focuses more, perhaps, on price or knowledge. Now, imagine if we map your whole organisation using an Organisation Motivational Map, and find that collectively your top three motivators – your top three employee drivers – are, say, Defender, Director and Star. How does this impact your work and delivery? Profoundly: you want and expect creativity from the employees – and they may agree that that's what they do – but beneath the collective surface, their real wants are for 'standards', 'authority', and 'respect' (just to use the first words in the sequences in Figure 6.2). It's possible for staff to have creative skills sets, but we find that over time that it is not enough; people default to doing what they want to do and rationalise that tendency. So whilst management is expecting 80% of time to be filled with being creative for customers – and things started that way –the motivational 'drag' means eventually 80% of time will be preoccupied with standards, authority and respect. And, of course, this works in reverse: suppose that 'standards'[6] are your key value, but your staff motivational profile is Creator, Spirit and Friend, then standards become far more difficult to accomplish.

Thus, 'values and consistency' are on the one hand about ensuring the accountability of every member of the organisation to walk the talk, and be held responsible for promoting and living the values. There can be no exceptions here. But also, consistency means taking a look at the motivational profile of the organisation (Figure 6.3) to see whether the motivators of the individuals and teams stack up.

We are not doing a full study of the Organisation Motivational Map here, but this is an abbreviated but typical data table from one that 'crunches' all the numbers that the individual Maps produce. Handily, we see the overall profile of the organisation (a sample of nearly 200 employees represented in these numbers), which is 69% motivated. Importantly, we see the rank order of motivators for the whole organisation (the top three being Searcher, Expert and Spirit in that order), and beneath that we see the profile for each individual team.

Activity 6.4

Look at the team called the leaders – these are the senior management team. What do you notice about their motivational profile as a team, versus the profile of the whole organisation?[7] And second, what do you notice about their motivational score?[8]

Now consider that this is a services company specialising in the production of accurate data. It is attempting to re-invent itself, and become more than just a 'data' company. To that end its recent values are: that they believe in being exploratory,

Top Motivator	Organisation Motivation Score:	69%
Second Motivator	Range of Scores :	10.5
Third Motivator	Change Index Score:	66%
Lowest Motivator	RAG:	31-31-38

Team Name	Searcher	Expert	Spirit	Defender	Creator	Builder	Star	Friend	Director	Motivation Audit %
Operations	736	675	665	611	677	563	477	552	444	72%
Public Sector	483	363	465	358	409	397	346	287	312	71%
B2B	365	293	256	306	283	331	256	191	239	69%
Customer Service	567	531	468	515	430	359	355	412	323	67%
Leaders	229	199	188	172	161	177	178	164	152	60%
Strategy	101	99	86	91	77	59	71	82	54	66%
B2C	102	84	90	68	81	76	67	59	93	72%
Scoring Totals	2626	2273	2271	2163	2150	2019	1795	1771	1652	

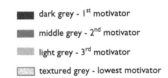

dark grey - 1st motivator

middle grey - 2nd motivator

light grey - 3rd motivator

textured grey - lowest motivator

Figure 6.3 Organisational data table showing teams

perceptive, dissatisfied, accurate. (Notice, once again, how easy it is to begin with creating noun-type lists; more exactly here of course they are adjectival!)

The question now, then, is that given what they do – producing highly accurate high-tech data and information (their mission) – are their guiding values likely to be supported by their motivational profile?

Activity 6.5

What do you think? Do the three dominant motivators of Searcher, Expert and Spirit (and perhaps their fourth, Defender) help or hinder the achievement of their values of being exploratory, perceptive, dissatisfied, accurate?

Our own view is that this motivational profile is a very good fit; these values will resonate with staff and they will want to embody and live them. Before leaving this topic, let's briefly look at why.

Let's ask ourselves which motivator, if any, most promotes or exhibits each one of these four values. First, being exploratory? The Spirit is the *exploratory* – indeed, entrepreneurial – motivator par excellence. Why? Because autonomy is always exploratory! We may work as a team, but we don't need to; we can go beyond that, and – exploring – press out on our own.

What about *perceptive*? Well, perception is about insight, understanding and relevance and to achieve all these three things requires skill, or … expertise. Thus, having the Expert motivator in the top three is certainly going to assist with realising this value.

Now *dissatisfied* – what an extraordinary and unusual value![9] What really is at the root of having dissatisfaction as a value? Surely, it is the desire to avoid complacency, habituation, and all that this leads to: namely, a failure to serve the current needs of the clients. In short, dissatisfaction is another way of expressing a constant – not a one-off – desire to make a difference for the client or customer. To want to make that difference, then, is to have the Searcher in our profile, which we do.

Finally, *accurate*: this could be argued to be another dimension of precision or exactness, but it is also, we feel, a quality of stability. When one is 'accurate', then one is on unshakeable ground, one is stable, and one is right. And that is a hunger that the Defender[10] motivator promotes.

What we are saying here, and what we found working in this organisation, was that the values and the motivators were consistent and mutually reinforcing, and so employees were incredibly engaged with their work and the organisation. Quite apart from all the productivity stats and the commercial success of this organisation, one other highlight of the Organisation Motivational Map is the fact that they are 69% motivated: the approximate average for an organisation of their size we have found to be somewhere in the 55–60% range. So the extra energy and productivity this company has is impressive.

We now come to look at the four skills we identified in Chapter 5. How we improve the abilities of our managers, so that they can truly become engaging managers, in the four areas of: cognitive and perceptual, interpersonal, presentational, and motivational skills? The most obvious thing is, firstly, to define them in a little more detail, or break them down into component parts, and then audit the staff. Figure 5.5 could be used simultaneously both by the boss of the engaging manager, and as a self-evaluation by the engaging manager, and their scores compared to see what areas of agreement there are, and where views diverge. In any case, the key thing is to set in train a programme which enables the manager to be at least an 8/10 in all four skill areas. Let's expand the skill set, then, but make it manageable by only including three subskills for each major heading.

Activity 6.6

Study Figure 6.4 and complete your own self-assessment of the 12 subskills identified. Ideally, your own manager or boss might like to give you their view of your skill set and how able you are, but if that is not possible or prudent, ask a trusted colleague to give you the feedback. Compare the two scores for each subskill. Differences should be analysed closely. Do you tend to over- or under-rate yourself? What level of score do you really need to be at to achieve what you want?

So far, so good. We have conducted a mini-training needs analysis and identified areas for improvement. We seem to be on track to be able to equip the engaging manager, but at this point in our narrative we need to point out a fatal flaw in what has gone before, and this debate to date: namely, there is a missing aspect to the whole development of the engaging manager, without which we believe it is not possible to have one. What is this missing aspect? As we discussed in our earlier book on Mapping Motivation and its chapter on leadership,[11] it is not the skill set, but the personal quality of self-awareness. In our earlier book we talked of the four dimensions[12] of self-awareness and the five ways[13] to generate more of it. Of those five ways, two are especially relevant here: acquiring quality feedback from external sources, and using diagnostic tools (and Motivational Maps happens to be a great example of one) to find out more about ourselves. And, as it happens, the Maps can allow both these things to happen simultaneously in an ingenious and exciting new application of Map technology.

		SCORE OUT OF 10		
SKILL	ABLE TO...	SELF	MANAGER	ACTIONPOINTS
Cognitive and Perceptual	Simplify complexity			
	Envision and strategize			
	Innovate and problem solve			
Interpersonal	Empathize, appreciate, use non verbal communication			
	Listen and make decisions			
	Negotiate			
Presentational	Communicate effectively as individuals and groups			
	Persuade and influence			
	Be confident and assured and instil these qualities in others			
Motivational	Understand and use Motivational Maps			
	Energize, enthuse, engage others			
	Reward appropriately			

Figure 6.4 12 subskill sets for the engaging manager

Before coming on to this application we need to stress, briefly, why self-awareness is so critically important.

Activity 6.7

Take time out here. Think about it: why is self-awareness so critically important if we are to develop engaging managers? How do you develop or improve your own self-awareness? Out of 10, how self-aware are you? What help do you need?

There are two primary reasons. The first is that without self-awareness we really cannot improve our own situation and performance; self-awareness calls us to audit ourselves, and having taken stock, to do something about it. The leader who is not self-aware is always attempting to solve today's challenges with yesterday's old and out-of-date self, the self that hasn't moved on in terms of knowledge, skills, experience and general capacity. Why would it, if it weren't aware that it needed to? Second, and perhaps as importantly, lack of self-awareness in terms of being an engaging manager specifically, has to be fatal: we have already established that we are requiring (advanced) interpersonal and motivational skills (to mention only two) in such a manager. How can one exhibit empathy, or negotiate effectively, or energise others if one is not aware of one's own state and condition? It's simply impossible. So, we need all organisations that are serious about creating engaging managers to consider the issue of self-awareness – as tricky as it is to define or measure even. But here is a major help – Motivational Maps!

Quality feedback, it turns out, is possibly the most powerful way known to humans to facilitate enhanced self-awareness, and most readers of this book will have heard of 360° Feedback (or 360° Appraisal), Put simply, this is the systematic method by which employees at certain, regular intervals receive feedback on their performance from a variety of sources: not just their own line manager, but often their colleagues, their subordinates, and even from clients and suppliers, depending on the nature of the organisation. In one obvious sense this has to be a no-brainer: what could be better than someone receiving all this feedback – surely, their performance must improve? You are certainly giving each individual an 'all-round perspective'.[14] Yet for all the hype there are several reasons why 360° Feedback needs to be approached with a long spoon.

The first is the time: it is incredibly time consuming (and so incredibly costly) to set up and run a proper 360° Feedback process. Second, 360° Feedback can become a sad substitute for the real management – engaging management – of employees; instead of managers directly communicating with or holding employees to account, they can use the 360° Feedback as a way of providing negative feedback, whilst at the same time absolving themselves of responsibility for it. Third, the process can sometimes can easily be subverted into one of point-scoring and game-playing within an organisation, and one main manifestation of this is when the feedback itself simply becomes a form of necessary 'box ticking'. And fourth, in order to set up a trustworthy 360° Feedback system – which is to say, one that is reliable, valid and credible – almost requires a PhD! What one has to understand in order to do this is not your average run-of-the-mill type of competence or understanding. That said, however, the principle that getting feedback from a wide variety of sources is sound. What if Motivational Maps could provide just such 360° Feedback? Fortunately, it can, and can do so quite simply, cheaply[15] and effectively.

The key to doing this is to adapt the Motivational Team Map.[16] Normally, the Team Map charts the motivational profile of each member of the team. But what if we were to ask the employee (E) to complete a Motivational Map *and* then ask the relevant people working with E to complete a Map, not as themselves, but as they perceive E to be; in other words, based on their perception of E. How do they perceive E as E? This can provide fascinating insights not only into E's self-perception, but of colleagues' perception – or misperception – of her.

Instructions to the relevant 'feedbackers', in our example the MD, the Admin, the Support and the Ops colleagues, as well as a critical supplier to the organisation, might go like this:

> We want you to give YOUR perceptions of E. We are NOT asking you to try and predict how you think E might respond; instead we want you to focus on what she does and says based on what you know of E. Based on your interactions with her, what do you feel, out of the two statements offered, best represents what would be E's preferences or priorities? How strong do you feel each statement would need to be to accurately reflect E's Leadership style and approach?

Activity 6.8

Looking at Figure 6.5, what three observations would you make on the data it provides?

Before discussing the meaning of this table we need to be clear about why this is so significant. First, because motivation is the primary asset of success in any work situation. So what we are getting here are five (there could be more or less) very relevant colleagues' views on how E operates at a motivational level. We can compare this with her own view, and we can also see at what intensity of energy, or motivation, she is working at. And, two more points are important: first, that this only takes 12 minutes of time per person to complete, and then all Maps can be automatically and instantly collated into one Team Map data table; the full result can be seen on one page! Second, the expertise needed to understand it is relatively simple, although complexity can be built in if necessary.

Name	Searcher	Spirit	Defender	Friend	Expert	Director	Star	Creator	Builder	Motivation Audit			
										%	1	2	3
MD on E	19	20	27	29	15	20	15	18	17	75%	8	8	3
E	35	28	14	23	18	18	16	11	17	61%	8	2	7
Admin on E	34	26	16	15	29	11	17	18	14	83%	8	9	8
Support on E	20	22	21	19	20	21	20	18	19	50%	5	5	5
Ops on E	25	14	23	22	22	18	21	21	14	80%	8	8	8
Supplier on E	19	20	25	18	19	22	20	20	17	43%	5	3	4
Total	152	130	126	126	123	110	109	106	98	65%			

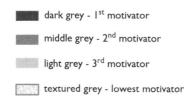

dark grey - 1st motivator

middle grey - 2nd motivator

light grey - 3rd motivator

textured grey - lowest motivator

Figure 6.5 360° Feedback table for E

To be equally clear, of course: we are not covering all the areas that a typical 360° Feedback would cover; but, we are covering the single most important thing. And in covering it much else will emerge as the data is itself actioned in feedback to the client. Keep in mind the 80/20 principle and we may be fairly sure that this process, whilst capturing only a small amount of the potential data, can account for a massive amount of the transformational effect. So less is more.

What, then, do we see from these individuals within the Team Map format (not an actual team of course but several perspectives on one individual)? We see that E's own perception of herself is that she is motivated by – in rank order – Searcher (making a difference), Spirit (being autonomous) and Friend (belonging). Now for our three points (although we could explore 20 here!):

1. Her boss, MD, is only perceptually aware of one (Friend) of her motivators. Serious or what?
2. No-one correctly anticipates all three of her motivators; the nearest is the person on Admin who sees two; the rest only guess one.
3. Her supplier – a critical organisational contact – is clueless: not knowing what motivates or even what most demotivates her.

If we go on, we see as well that Supplier and Support see her as quite demotivated (43% and 50% respectively), whereas her boss and the Admin person rate her more highly. Is this because, especially with the boss, she works more closely with them, or that she puts on more of an act? Whatever the reason, this can provide the basis for a fruitful discussion. As can the fact that whereas E feels that she has little freedom in the role (2/10 score), her Admin sees her as being very autonomous (9/10)! On the other hand, Support sees her Spirit as 5/10. This truly is a wonderful conflict of mixed perceptions, which, with a licensed practitioner of Maps, can be fed back in an entirely constructive way.

It would take too long to talk about all that was fed back to E but the results are worth commenting on. E, from being relatively directionless, goalless and non-accountable, moved to understanding and committing to: attending to details, 'planning backwards' (in other words having the end in mind and seeing the steps necessary to achieve that end state or goal), reviewing and monitoring her staff more thoroughly whilst accepting more accountability, and finally to realise that strategies, processes and procedures were not set in stone, but required ongoing reviews and updates. All in all, then, a pretty enormous shift for someone who was underperforming, proving problematic, but now through Maps and its 360° Feedback process was coming back as a serious contributor to the work of the organisation. In short E was becoming engaged, and soon to practise as an engaging manager.[17]

MacLeod commented[18] that '…We need to have honest conversations and sometimes difficult conversations. We need to talk to employees about "what really gets you out of bed". We really need to understand people.' So we argue that this process of using Maps for 360° Feedback is just such a process par excellence: for understanding where somebody is coming from and at the same time from where we are too in relationship to them. To be able to do this is truly remarkable.

Thus, in this chapter, we have indicated how we would go about creating the right values and consistency, how we would audit the necessary skills, and how to develop the necessary self-awareness in the engaging manager, without which they will certainly fail. It remains, then, to consider the issue of reward strategies.

Rewards are an interesting concept, especially considering the issue of engaging managers and what such managers do. Why, surely, they must be rewarding employees all the time?[19] For the principle reason why we perform is to be rewarded; that is what we understood as children, that was the deal with parents – be a good boy or girl and be rewarded for it. But interesting as this idea is, we find that two of the best books[20] on engagement in recent times do not even have the word 'reward' listed in their indices. There is of course a lot of talk about compensation, benefits, culture, cultures of well-being, diversity and inclusiveness, and similar, but less, it would seem, on WHAT,[21] actually, are the specific rewards that people want?[22]

As Kenneth W. Thomas[23] remarked: 'You need a diagnostic framework to point you toward what's most likely to make a difference and to save you from having to try motivational solutions in an inefficient, hit-or-miss way'. Exactly: to save you from hit-or-miss ways, and all that waste, and at the same time to be able to generate a true 'rainbow' of rewards. If we consider that a rainbow has nine colours (including infra-red and ultra-violet!), then we realise that the nine types of motivators all produce different coloured rewards (Figure 6.6).

What are, then, the specific 'rainbow' rewards for the engaging managers? First, the engaging manager can only reward effectively if they know their employees' motivators, and if they act on that information.

The engaging manager rewards[24] by . . .

It should be clear from Figure 6.7 that this requires considerable versatility on the part of the engaging manager. But no-one said it was easy! And, of course, we all tend to focus on the aspect of motivation that aligns with our

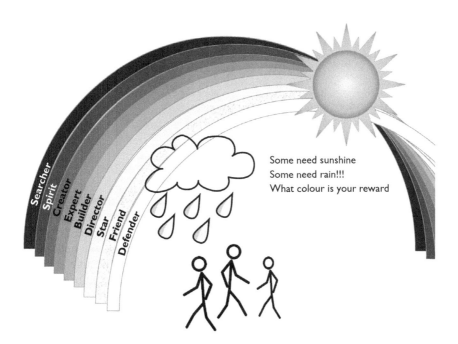

Figure 6.6 Motivational 'rainbow' of rewards

Searcher	Focusing on the big Why? Purpose and mission Ensuring a fit-for-purpose physical and technical environment Providing streams of quality, and customer feedback
Spirit	Allowing employees to control aspects of their work, space Delegating effectively and holding accountable Removing red tape and bureaucracy
Creator	Avoiding too much routine Presenting challenging goals or problems to solve Rewarding creative solutions
Expert	Providing ongoing, regular training and coaching Ensuring regular technical tips and updates available Encouraging employees to share their expertise
Builder	Linking targets to financial outcomes and rewards Creating a competitive environment Offering perks, small or otherwise, as tangible incentives
Director	Expanding their scope of control Recommending career development training,especially leadership. Promoting them
Star	Giving them a significant job title or description Treating them as if they were an 'insider' Appreciating their work and reputation
Friend	Focusing on team dynamics Asking them for their opinion Providing lots of social opportunities to mix
Defender	Being clear on long-term plans and expectations Ensuring systems and processes are effective and in place Reducing clutter

Figure 6.7 Engaging manager 'rainbow' rewards

own preferences; accordingly, we often fail to see how it is for someone at the other end of the rainbow, as it were. The danger, then, is always to imagine that people are just like us, when in fact all experience shows – along with a moment's thought – that they are not. One thing we find helpful at this point is to become aware of the essential communicative task that the engaging manager needs to embrace even before the allocation and distribution of specific rewards. In other words, if the rewards are *what* we deliver, then the communication(s) of it are the *how* of the matter – the exciting buzz that resonates with the employee and makes them want to get into gear.[25]

What this means is a verbal orientation that we adopt, and which is skewed towards the preferences of the employee. We say 'preferences' because keep in mind that each employee usually has three motivational preferences, any one of which may be the 'meeting' point where the engaging nmanager can connect with their employee.

Activity 6.9

Clearly, Figure 6.8 and its 'key languages' is a tool that is meant to be used in real situations. This predicates knowing what another's motivational profile is, ideally via a Motivational Map. But consider a colleague, customer or client you know fairly well. What are their top one or two motivators? Try introducing some 'key language' into your next conversation with them that matches their profile. What do you notice?

If you spot an uptake, an enthusiasm, a lift in excitement and commitment, then you are certainly impacting one of their key motivators. Thus, in learning the language of motivation as we have been doing throughout this book, we are also learning to notice more: motivation is energy, so when we speak we spot the words we use that generate more positive energy, and so that information enables us to identify motivators and build the conversation towards a mutually desirable outcome.

We have, then, in Chapters 5 and 6, covered some enormously important elements of being an engaging manager – an effective leader. At this point we need to emphasise the importance of understanding in developing such a

MOTIVATOR	Key Language will be deployed around ...
Searcher	Big picture, why we do what we do, feedback
Spirit	Empowerment, assigning control to, independence
Creator	Big, small problems, innovative, unique solutions
Expert	Deep knowledge, skills, learning, personal expertise
Builder	Goals, targets, results, competitive practices, 'be first'
Director	Leadership, management, personal responsibilities
Star	Reputation, structure, personal importance
Friend	Teamwork, personal involvement, social events
Defender	Long-term security, plans, embedding systems

Figure 6.8 Motivator key languages

manager: we are not presenting systematic checklists of things to do with a sort of guarantee of 'bingo!' if they are done. Moving people forward is a developmental process requiring sensitivity, patience, resources and insight. At all times we have tried to stress what the actual issues are and what can be done about them; in these two chapters especially, then, going through the activities is vital if one is to get a real sense of the problems we may encounter.

Notes

1 Simon Sinek, *Start with Why*, Penguin (2009). More explicitly, Sinek says,

> Making it more difficult for ourselves, we remind ourselves of our values by writing them on a wall ... as nouns. Integrity. Honesty. Innovation. Communication, for example. But nouns are not actionable. They are things. You can't build systems or develop incentives around those things. It's nearly impossible to hold people accountable to nouns.

2 Bob Garratt, *The Fish Rots from the Head*, HarperCollins (1997).
3 Here are some ideas – and we can debate them a long time. They are not right or wrong, but they are superior to a list of nouns, especially because they require specific actions: Integrity might be: to always act in a way that is honest, fair, kind and truthful; Consistency might be: to behave consistently with our words, to insist on being accountable for our words and actions; Creativity might be: to initiate challenges, to embrace innovation, to be curious; Leadership might be: to lead with passion, integrity and self-awareness; Empowerment might be: to inspire others through my example, to delegate effectively, to express confidence in others through words and deeds; Commitment might be: to do the best I can all the time I can.
4 Sinek maintains that their choice of U2 in a promotional iPod partnership was a perfect fit, whereas using Celine Dion, who had sold more records than U2, wasn't. U2 were edgy, pushing boundaries – like Apple; Celine Dion was mainstream and so 'conventional'.
5 We are not going to do all these, since we think what we are asking is clear. But to take the first word, 'fairness', then that might become: 'we treat all people kindly and without prejudice'.
6 And expressed as a verb, standards might be: we always provide a polite, proactive excellent level of service, or, our products are 99.9% defect-free.
7 We notice that their profile mirrors the profile of the whole organisation. This can be good or bad – so, good in that one is aligned with the majority 'feeling and desires'; but bad if there is too much conformity and groupthink. In this case, and in the majority of cases, it is good because (as is actually the case with this company) the senior people do speak the 'language' of their employees. As a sidebar, note that all the teams share the Searcher – making a difference – as their number one motivator. This is unusual, but in this case does suggest a deep alignment of purpose.
8 That the senior people are the least motivated of all the company teams! This is invariably a bad sign since staff take their cues from senior people, and ultimately this will prove – if not corrected – a drag on the whole organisation's motivational and so engagement levels.
9 Though see Chapter 8 and Figure 8.9 for the centrality of 'dissatisfaction' in the change process; it is paradoxical that in order to be 'satisfied' with what one is doing, one has to be simultaneously 'dissatisfied'!

10 However, keep in mind we are only presenting a partial analysis here, for the sake of illustration, but one clear and apparent point that needs examining is that the Searcher and Defender motivators are in conflict, as the desire for change is inhibited by the desire for stability; this can be of course a dynamic tension.

11 Chapter 8, James Sale, *Mapping Motivation*, Routledge (2016).

12 The four dimensions or levels are: physical, mental, emotional and spiritual.

13 The five ways to generate more self-awareness are through: acquiring quality feedback, using diagnostic profiling tools, starting a journal, challenging yourself beyond your 'comfort zone', and using your imagination to visualise ideal states that intensify the short-fall in the present.

14 A phrase used by a leading UK expert on 360° Feedback: Elva R Ainsworth. Her book, *360° Feedback: A Transformational Approach*, Panoma Press (2016), is an extremely insightful and valuable contribution in this field.

15 This application is still in its early days of experimentation within the Maps community, but anecdotal evidence from practitioners using this methodology suggests that it is some 70% less in terms of cost, and even better still in terms of time saved.

16 The first Mapper to do this and to whom we are indebted for this idea and case study of E is Mark Turner: http://bit.ly/2pe2iAH.

17 We have not explored this, but E's new approach to 'detail' and 'processes' was not just driven by an appreciation of what her true motivators were, but also borne of a self-awareness that the Defender motivator – the one particularly driven to detail and processes – was her second lowest, and this 'Achilles' heel' needed addressing.

18 The MacLeod Report, David MacLeod et al., *Engaging for Success: Enhancing Performance through Employee Engagement*, Office of Public Sector Information (2009).

19 'When rewards are perceived as recognition for competence, they increase intrinsic motivation, probably because they fulfil a psychological need.' Amar Fall and Patrice Russell, Compensation and Work Motivation: Self-Determination Theory and the Paradigm of Motivation through Incentives, *The Oxford Handbook of Work Engagement, Motivation and Self-Engagement Theory*, edited Marylène Gagné, Oxford University Press (2014).

20 David Bowles and Cary Cooper, *The High Engagement Work Culture*, Palgrave Macmillan (2012) and Jacob Morgan, *The Employee Experience Advantage*, Wiley (2017). Whilst not specifically highlighting the concept of reward strategies as we understand them, these books do of course provide their 'take' on what rewards might be. To consider Morgan's view: this is very much about employees wanting fairness, feedback, and feeling valued, and also thriving when 'diversity and inclusion', 'health and wellness', and 'being part of a team' are dominant.

21 HOW we reward them is also important; and the HOW we do things is invariably a function of our value systems; hence the importance that most engagement experts attribute to the value system in an organisation: that the value of 'fairness', for example, is perceived to be adhered to. Clearly, if employees feel that the distribution of rewards is unfair, then apart from the small minority of beneficiaries of that unfairness, staff will become disengaged.

22 We need to be clear here that we are not simplistically expecting a direct reward pattern of the 'if-you-do-this-then-you-get-that' type or variety of transaction. As Deci observed:

> Indeed, research has shown that when employees get focused on rewards, their tendency is to take the shortest path to the outcomes which can easily be manifest

as cheating, gaming the system, and sacrificing the long-term interests of the company in the service of short-term goals. This contamination effect is readily apparent in the corporate world, perhaps most infamously in the Enron saga

Edward L. Deci and Richard M. Ryan, The Importance of Universal Needs for Understanding Motivation in the Workplace, *The Oxford Handbook of Work Engagement, Motivation and Self-Engagement Theory*, edited Marylène Gagné, Oxford University Press (2014). As soon as rewards appear contingent and manipulative – as opposed to being freely and fairly distributed on merit – then the gaming of the system will commence.

23 In his compelling book, *Intrinsic Motivation at Work*, Kenneth W. Thomas identifies four intrinsic rewards: Meaningfulness, Choice, Competence and Progress. If you have been reading this book carefully you will immediately spot that these four 'intrinsic motivators' correspond, more or less, with our Searcher, Spirit, Expert and Creator: the top four motivators in our Maslow Hierarchy. However, that's not the same as addressing all nine motivators, although it could be argued that as we descend the motivational pyramid the motivators do take on what appears to be a more 'extrinsic' aspect. Indeed, the next one below Expert is Builder, money! But the difference here is that we are arguing that whilst under a conventional view of motivators they are either intrinsic or extrinsic, the so-called extrinsic motivators in our model are actually intrinsic for those employees who have them. This is a break-through perception. All nine motivators are potentially intrinsic, therefore.

24 A cautionary warning to these ideas must always be: according to the resources available to the organisation and the competence and abilities of the employees. There is no good, for example, to be had in providing financial rewards in excess of the targets achieved, or in allowing the scope of control of an employee to exceed their ability to handle it.

25 Again: artificially, mechanically, superficially applied, no words work. If the engaging manager is not himself or herself excited by, for example, the big picture or why, they will hardly persuade the employee to be motivated by it.

Chapter 7

Motivational organisational maps and strategic narrative

We return now to the MacLeod Report's 'Strategic Narrative' enabler of employee engagement. As MacLeod expressed it:

> A strong narrative that provides a clear, shared vision for the organisation is at the heart of employee engagement. Employees need to understand not only the purpose of the organisation they work for but also how their individual role contributes to that purpose.
>
> MacLeod (2009)[1]

It is our considered view that the more intangible, invisible and 'airy-fairy' an element of organisational development is (and specifically in relation to employee engagement), the more likely it is to be of paramount importance. In a way it is easy to see how 'enabling managers' contribute – almost by definition – to employee engagement; but a strategic narrative? Isn't this just something for boffins at head office who love producing pages of paperwork and who simultaneously like to consider this 'real' work? Sadly, it would be easy to become cynical, but the reality is that even the engaging managers will in the end run out of steam if there is no 'strategic narrative' underpinning their efforts, strengthening their resolve and fortifying their motivations.

The truth is that the seriously important things in life all tend to be intangibles, and invisibles – like values, beliefs, emotions, motivations, dreams – precede, and so drive, the outcomes in the concrete world we experience. For this reason, it is important to pay attention to them, and not, as so many executives do, just consider the tangibles: the revenues, the profits, the assets and all the 'things' we can list on or deduce from a balance sheet. It is the lack of attention – and so respect – paid to people generally that is at the root of so much disengagement and disaffection in the work place. Let's just consider, then, for a moment why this 'strategic narrative' is so critical.

First, notice that it is a 'strategic narrative' and not a 'narrative strategy'. The point here is that the key word is 'narrative', the noun, which is qualified by the lesser word, 'strategic', which is an adjective. As we quoted before:[2] 'narrative may be regarded as a primary act of mind'. Once we unpack the significance of what that means, then we are on our way to 'getting' why this is so crucial.

Activity 7.1

What does 'narrative may be regarded as a primary act of mind' mean to you? Why might it be important? Is its meaning confined to just organisational life and employment only? In what other areas of life might it be applicable?

A good and simple synonym for 'narrative' is 'story'. We discussed this in Chapter 2. Stories are a primary act of mind, which means that they are a primary way in which we interpret reality. It is not through so-called 'facts' that we understand our lives, but through the stories that incorporate them. We weave, as it were, the facts or our interpretation of the facts, into some kind of cloth or garment that we then wear as our understanding of reality. And we need this garment in order to survive, to stay warm. Without a story – stories – our lives make no sense. Indeed, ultimately our lives become meaningless, and this, when it happens, causes severe psychological problems for those experiencing it: loss of self-esteem, depression, suicide and so on. And what is true for the individual applies to the team and to the whole organisation. An organisation without a compelling story has almost certainly a short shelf-life, and no matter how big will begin to disintegrate from within. At this moment of writing just such a situation is emerging in America with one of the USA's biggest corporations: GE.[3] Under CEO Jack Welch it had a compelling (though, with hindsight, possibly flawed) narrative, but for the last 16 years or so it has just grown by seemingly random acquisitions and so has lost its story.

The organisational story, then, we are wanting to talk about is the story about what we do – the mission – the story about where we are going – the vision, and absolutely crucially how the employees contribute to that 'doing' and that 'going'. Finally, there is also the narrative about not only what we do – the mission – but how we do what we do: namely, our values, which inform everything, and which define the kind of people we really are – our character, as it were. This last point links into the final MacLeod enabler integrity,[4] which we shall be considering in the next chapter.

This can all sound rather abstract, but the key thing to get is that the employee must a. be clear about what the organisation is trying to achieve, and b. must see how they fit in and contribute meaningfully to it. Communication, then, is once again vital.

One last point before we consider how Maps can help inform this process: the word 'strategic' qualifies our 'narrative'. What is strategic? The word comes from the ancient Greek word, '*strategos*', which was a military commander or general in the field of battle. Thus, strategy is about the art of winning battles, which is about winning territory, be it physical, emotional or intellectual. What we want through strategy is to occupy a space, a territory, a market that is ours, and we want to occupy it securely; thus, to do so, we need to have an 'army' that is motivated, committed, engaged and highly skilled and knowledgeable; in other words, an effective army. And if we think about it in terms of an army, it becomes pretty clear how all the different sections of an army must be encouraged, co-ordinated and deployed in a way which maximises their impact, not just in a particular skirmish or battle, but in the overall war. The strategy is just 'seeing' how the different parts must fit and cohere if one is to optimise one's strengths – and face the challenges (uncertainties) that are bound (certain) to arrive. Strategy *is* dealing with the uncertainty of impending disruptions! A story, then, is vital in enabling every individual see how they help 'make it happen'; there is a strong connection between what they are doing and the outcomes for the whole organisation somewhere down the line. There is the famous, if apocryphal, NASA story that goes: President John F. Kennedy[5] visited NASA headquarters in 1961. As he toured the building, he introduced himself to a janitor who was mopping the floor and asked him what he did at NASA. The janitor replied, 'I'm helping put a man on the moon!' That is strategic narrative in action: the employee at the lowest level buys into the big picture and sees how he or she is helping. Notice, too, how the top person takes an interest in the views of the lowest one: empowering leadership.

If this seems fanciful, consider Jonah Sachs' comments to the effect that 'all wars are story wars'[6]– so stories are what compel people to wage war and to want wage war, and the strategic aspect of it is what sustains their efforts; for we believe in our stories when they are authentic, sincere and relevant to us. In short, stories motivate us because they make sense of life for us. And of course, how they motivate us, as stories, can be in one of nine ways. Most obviously, since they give us meaning, they appeal to the Searcher motivator where meaningfulness or purpose is most extreme. But stories also contain within them the seeds of the other motivators too (Figure 7.1).

It should be obvious from the above that not only is this issue of stories relevant to strategic narratives of the organisation as a whole, but should also emerge in their marketing too; for marketing campaigns focus on espoused values, which are exactly what we talking about when we say, 'potentially showing'. So Dove's 'Real Beauty'[7] campaign – 'Truth is beauty and the truth is, everyone is beautiful' – was appealing to the core values of truth and beauty. We see both these values reflected in two of our motivators, the Defender and the Creator. Similarly, but moving into politics, Barack Obama's 2008 presidential campaign – 'working hard together, we can solve our problems' – focussed on the two values of wholeness and perfection; these also are related to two of our motivators, the Searcher and the Expert.

This is not a book about marketing and how to craft strategic narratives – stories – that catch the public imagination and drive sales or win votes, but it is a book about how, if we want to engage our employees, our stories must appeal to them and be something that they buy into; and they buy into it because the story becomes part of their story. Another way of expressing this is: the employees become co-creators of the story. They welcome and they love the opportunity to

Stories about	Potentially Showing	Aligned Motivator
Making sense of experience	meaning/wholeness	Searcher
Empowerment and release	autonomy/simplicity	Spirit
Creativity and play	beauty/uniqueness	Creator
Knowledge and expertise	mastery/perfection	Expert
Resourcing and money	richness/competitiveness	Builder
Control and leadership	power/justice	Director
Personal excellence and shining	recognition/importance	Star
Belonging and community	friendship/collaboration	Friend
Security and planning	safety/truth	Defender

Figure 7.1 Stories and motivators

be so involved, and in a vital and important sense it is the employees who continue and extend the story. Without them, the story goes nowhere; indeed, becomes a dead or lifeless story.

There are two aspects of this, then, that we should now consider. One should be obvious: we need to consider our organisational story and ask ourselves: what are the two or three key values that underpin it? And having established that, set the values against the motivational profile of the organisation (obviously, this methodology works at the team level too).

Activity 7.2

Consider the organisation that you work for, or once worked for, or an organisation that is a client or supplier, and which you know reasonably well. Identify: a. what is their story or strategic narrative?[8] b. what values underpin that narrative? And finally, c. knowing what you now about Motivational Maps and the motivators, do you think that the typical motivators of most of the staff reflect and reinforce the values in the strategic narrative, or work against it (Figure 7.2)?

Clearly, what we think are the values may well be a false estimation, and what we think are the typical motivators – the 'invisible' – may be even more of an incorrect assessment; but we ask you to consider this question precisely

Strategic Narrative:			
2 or 3 Values espoused in the narrative:			
Motivators that might support the values:			

Figure 7.2 Narrative, values and motivators

because in doing so, the need to actually find out by mapping the organisation becomes very apparent.

And this leads on, nicely, to our second aspect. Bizarrely, we jump from stories and values and all that intangible stuff to discussing key metrics. We made the point in Chapter 4 that staff surveys were not the best or most efficient way by which to measure engagement; we gave several reasons for this. However, the issue of metrics now comes to the fore as we discuss strategic narrative. What metrics should organisations use? This, of course, also takes us back to Chapter 1 and the seven steps to employee engagement: steps two and three – where are we now and what will be the measures? So, paradoxically, forget measuring engagement – at least directly through surveys; start measuring energy, and its outcomes. Clearly, this is always going to be sensitive and unique issue, contingent on the nature of the organisation itself. But that said, we think that there are seven key metrics to choose from, and that a good way forward is to use three of them in any given period. They are not all 'equal', some we rate more highly than others, and so we think we should give a more detailed breakdown of what we mean by each. But before we do, consider Activity 7.3.

Activity 7.3

We want to establish whether or not employees are truly engaged within an organisation, and we have decided NOT to use an employee or staff survey tool. What in your opinion would be good alternatives to this? List as many as you can think of. Which three are the most likely to be significant?

Let's consider each of these seven measures (Figure 7.3). First, and naturally, we think that the Organisational Motivational Map is actually the superior substitute for the annual staff survey that most organisations currently use. Furthermore, it can work just at team level too. But the reality is in our view that engagement is approximately 70% motivation and 30% behaviours;[9] thus, to measure in a snapshot how motivated employees are will correlate very

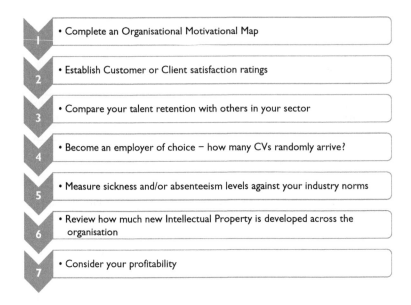

1 • Complete an Organisational Motivational Map

2 • Establish Customer or Client satisfaction ratings

3 • Compare your talent retention with others in your sector

4 • Become an employer of choice – how many CVs randomly arrive?

5 • Measure sickness and/or absenteeism levels against your industry norms

6 • Review how much new Intellectual Property is developed across the organisation

7 • Consider your profitability

Figure 7.3 Seven key metrics to establish employee engagement indirectly

closely with how engaged they are. The great advantage about using the Organisational Motivational Map, apart from its low cost, is that it is virtually impossible to 'game': there would be no point in doing so anyway, since the questions don't lend themselves to internal politics. Here we will have a definitive (albeit temporary, as motivators change over time) fix on the energy levels and direction of the organisation.

But we as experienced coaches or consultants do not want to spend all our time navel-gazing, re-arranging the deck chairs on the Titanic as icebergs hove into proximity! At the end of the day, what does employees being engaged, having high energy, mean? It means there will be a ripple effect of energy, and the beneficiaries of that ripple will first and foremost be the customer or the client. A key question for any organisation, any business, is *how*: how satisfied, how happy are customers and clients with what we are doing, with the service or products we supply to them and, critically, how we treat them? As has been observed many times: the primary business of a business is not to make a profit; that is a by-product of retaining happy customers. If our staff are motivated and engaged, our customers will feel it.

And another area where we as an organisation will feel it is in talent retention. To be competitive in our industry or sector we need to attract and retain the most talented people. Once, therefore, employees are engaged, the energy levels go palpably up and it feels good; in that scenario great people want to stay, and resist being lured away simply by the prospect of more money at the cost of working in a non-engaging sweat-shop. Quality of life – and work – is increasingly at a premium and the best organisations in the world are having to address this issue. But let's not forget as well that loss of talent is a huge cost to business. To put this in perspective, the American Bureau of National Affairs[10] reckons that the staff turnover rate in 2013 was 65% and would lead to a loss of $11 billion to US businesses! That is a pretty substantial loss.

Activity 7.4

Consider the following questions in Figure 7.4. Makes notes on your answers. Share your answers internally with someone you trust, first asking them to answer the questions. What picture emerges from your answers?

We have used the term 'talent' here since it is a term widely – apparently – understood.[11] But it should be clear that this whole issue, including recruitment, learning and development, and even contingency[12] planning is of paramount important and relevance to employee engagement.[13] This is just one of the seven main areas where we can evaluate how 'engaged' our employees are, and seek to make them more so.

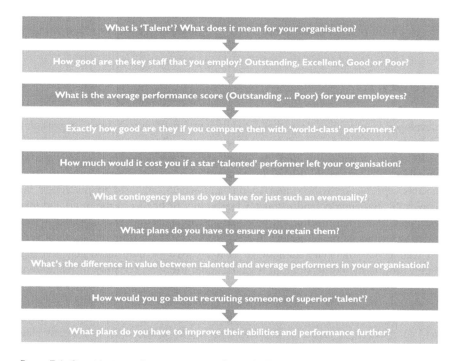

Figure 7.4 Considering and rating your employees' talent

Also, like attracts like, so it is not only in talent retention that the effect of engaged and motivated staff is felt. The fact is high-energy people are attracted to other high-energy people; as we say, like attracts like; and nobody much wants to go to a party and spend time in the kitchen with low-energy people. Word gets out. If you are an organisation with engaged staff and engaging managers, expect to receive unsolicited CVs from applicants keen to join your organisation whether you have advertised a job, or even have a vacancy, or not. Is the number of unsolicited CVs and enquiries landing on your desk increasing? If it is, then that is one indicator (but not a fool-proof one, and not enough alone) that your staff are increasingly engaged.

Measuring sickness and absenteeism[14] levels are a very clear way of measuring engagement,[15] as well of course as measuring loss. There are many aspects to this but David Bowles[16] makes the point that 'clear evidence ... would support what some long-established theories have put forward that absenteeism and similar behaviours are an effort by the workers to "level the playing field," to make up for what is *perceived to be an imbalance*'. Here specifically Bowles is referring to huge disparities in pay and remuneration and staff's perception of its unfairness – leading to their disengagement. The point, of course, is that when they are engaged, and not troubled by issues of 'unfairness', then their need to resort to absenteeism and sickness declines and attendance levels (as well, incidentally, as the lesser issue of punctuality) improve.

We come now to our sixth important measure of employee engagement: the development of Intellectual Property (IP) within the organisation. This sounds a curious one.

Activity 7.5

What does IP mean in and for your organisation? In what areas could it be developed? And why does the development of IP across your organisation indicate increasing levels of employee engagement?

IP is the opposite of land, buildings and physical property, which are all tangible; IP is intangible. It is the creation of ideas, processes, systems, trade secrets, special know-how and so on, and which can lead to protection via copyright, trademarks, and patents. Clearly, this IP begins in the mind and then becomes something useful and practical for organisations to adopt and, where there is serious value, to protect. But the important thing from our perspective is to realise that the generation of IP is a creative or innovative act, and that innovation is the cornerstone of organisational life, and certainly of its survival into the future.

Indeed, the only way to protect an organisation's future is to be constantly innovating, for as the cliché goes, change is accelerating, disruption is the norm, and so to accommodate this, organisations can no longer exist in a steady state of drift: they have to be disruptive – that is to say, innovative – themselves. But how can they do this without innovative employees?

Two points are, perhaps, worth considering here. The first is that in considering innovation we need to think beyond simply our product or service offering; in other words, beyond just what we 'do': the operational stuff. To take the main four areas of organisational life: finance, marketing/sales, operations and people (see Figure 1.8), then each of them is open to innovative new practices, albeit small initially, but which over time can produce competitive advantage. Second, the development of new ideas, new processes, new systems, better ways of doing things, is invariably, and by definition, the result of employing the 'best' people; for it is always the best people who come up with the best ideas and solutions, and that is why they are the best! Of course, everyone starts off a novice and a learner, but in the right environment can develop world-class capabilities (Figure 7.5).

Thus, whether the innovations are big shifts, huge discoveries, wholly new ways of doing things, or whether they are the result of kaisen-type[17] processes whereby small incremental improvements are constantly being made (which is a surer, more stable and process-orientated route), the question becomes: are you monitoring or reviewing how much new IP is being created by your employees across the whole organisation? If you employ the best people, there will be a continual increase in new IP; if you don't employ the best, then you might want to ask, why not? And what can

Figure 7.5 Creativity burning brightly

you do about it. If there is no new IP created within your organisation, then that would be a serious cause for concern.

Finally, we must address profitability, because everyone does, and in the last analysis, we know it is a critical factor; it is a practical demonstration of the fact that our organisation has added value to the world and been rewarded for that value. But also we do need to be wary of profitability, since it has the potential to subvert any organisation if it is made the 'god' of all our endeavours. For one thing obvious from the last 30 years with all the lay-offs, downsizing, outsourcing, rationalising, economising, and simply firing people, is that there have been valid reasons for doing so, which include reducing operating costs, improving organisational efficiency and productivity, and so the competitiveness of the organisation. There is sometimes – especially once one has been successful – 'bloat' that needs to be dealt with. But that said, where reducing operating costs is 'the god' just to bump up profits, then we get into that situation where staffing is cut to the bone and the customer experience suffers dramatically; there comes a point, then, when the organisational life itself is threatened by an overemphasis[18] on profitability at the expense of all else. And it should be noted at this point too that of course such an overemphasis becomes a palpable value statement within the organisation that absolutely will not speak to the majority of employees: it is in fact a very low-grade strategic narrative,[19] for it says, 'we only care about money'. We, therefore, would not usually consider profitability the ideal metric by which to establish employee engagement, but we also accept that it is important, and for some organisations may have to be part of the mix.

Activity 7.6

Given these seven metrics and what they mean, which three seem most important to you and your organisation. Which three metrics would you use? How will you go about implementing their usage?

In Chapter 2 we discussed the four enablers of employee engagement, and in Figure 2.1 we included 'visible, empowering leadership'. This phrase is the synonymous expression that is used to communicate the idea of a 'strategic narrative', and the reason it is used almost synonymously is because it is only through such leadership that a strategic narrative can be generated and communicated. Without the leadership, how will the strategic narrative be developed, communicated, shared, adopted and embraced? Leadership, then, is the vehicle of strategic narrative. Clearly, certain phrases and ideas – leadership, communication, narrative – keep recurring, and we keep returning to explore them further. But what is the difference between this 'visible, empowering leadership' and the 'engaging manager' that we discussed at length in Chapters 5 and 6?

In one sense no difference at all. We want engaging managers to be visible, empowering leaders and we want vice versa. But in another sense, there is an important distinction to be made, and this really revolves around levels of responsibility. The bigger the organisation the more potential levels of seniority there are, and this, if taken to extremes, is the essence of bureaucracy: layers and layers of management in which hair-splitting over who is responsible for what, *exactly*, takes months, if not years, of time to establish and refine. Given modern complexities, certainly three levels may not be sufficient to accommodate what a hierarchy of command needs to accomplish. But that said, it is usually pretty clear, when one breaks down what is going on, that there are in reality but three key levels:

Level 1: employees actually doing the work – operational staff DOING
Level 2: employees managing operational staff – middle managers PROCESSING
Level 3: employees leading everything – senior managers THINKING ('conceptualising')

And this returns us to our fundamental understanding of performance as outlined in Chapters 1 and 3. That 'direction' – going in the right direction – was vital to high performance, and that motivation (Figure 3.2) provided the serious WHY preceding or aligned with the direction of travel. At the end of the day we can consult and involve our employees, and that is a good thing, but the senior team, and in particular the CEO or MD, has to articulate the strategic narrative for the organisation. If they don't do so, the organisation is either destined to drift, or to be hijacked by other, negative narratives deriving from the staff themselves or competitor organisations.

So, if we consider now Figure 7.6 we can see, perhaps, what we are trying to explain. All leaders should be engaging managers, and engaging managers should be visionary leaders; and there is a clear overlap of skills at all levels. Note how at the very senior level the conceptual line majors on being in the 'senior' box, but senior people, too, need to have 'middle' capabilities – that is to say, interpersonal or 'engaging' skills. Furthermore, the conceptual line even crosses into the operational box. The idea that senior leaders never do operational work is mildly absurd, as is the idea that they never actually enter the work space, the factory floor, the assembly line. The very best senior people are always doing this.[20] And it is evident from the three lines – conceptual, interpersonal and technical – that the skills are not entirely compartmentalised. Even the operational staff probably need to have some interpersonal skills if they are to function at optimal levels, and one such interpersonal skill, much in demand these days, would be team working.

Thus, there is a fluidity in all of this, but given that, the overall picture is clear: at the very senior level, apart from some technical skills and knowledge, and hopefully advanced interpersonal (that is, engaging) skills, the leader needs conceptual skills. Conceptual skills are a posh way of saying 'thinking' skills: thinking through, for example, which customers, which segments, what behaviours, what resources, timings, communications we are going to identify, focus on, and utilise to achieve our vision, and, also, what is the strategic narrative of the organisation? Creating a storyline that encompasses the values, the vision and the mission of the organisation, incorporates its history and struggle, and clearly points to its

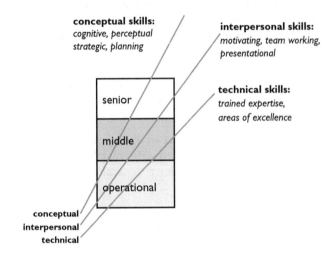

Figure 7.6 Three levels of an organisation: operational, middle, senior

destination. Sometimes the destination is beyond reach, but the story nevertheless inspires its accomplishment. A summary strapline of the '80s/'90s that was brilliantly effective in promoting the company and at the same time giving the employees an exciting and dynamic focus, was Bill Gates[21] of Microsoft's 'A computer on every desk and in every home'. The great thing about such a statement is its aspirational nature, which every employee can buy into, and furthermore get a quick 'return' from: every time a Microsoft product was sold, the statement was being more and more realised. How exciting was that? Or again we could cite the more recent Google's[22] reason for being: 'to organise the world's information and make it universally accessible and useful'. This has led Google to outperform companies like Microsoft in acquiring 'talent' for the organisation.

Visible, empowering leadership, then, provides a strong, strategic narrative about the organisation: where it's come from, where it is now, and where it aspires to go in the future. And it needs to be something staff can really associate with,[23] which deploys a common language throughout the organisation, and which is something that gives purpose and meaning to all activities within the business. Another way of putting this, according to Jacob Morgan, is creating a 'reason for being' that speaks to the employee's experience, and this will have four, easy to understand features as shown in Figure 7.7.

Activity 7.7

Consider whether your organisation follows the four features: does it focus on impact? Is it *not* centred purely on financial gain? Is there something big – virtually

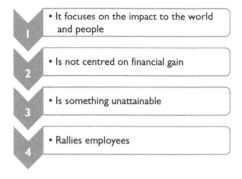

Figure 7.7 Four features of our core mission/narrative

impossible – that it is trying to do? And are staff really behind it? These questions can be dealt with in the privacy of one's own mind, but how much more effective will they be at board level, or if the senior team, or any project group within an organisation is asked to review them? They are a call to renewal and action.

It should be obvious from what we are saying here that focusing on the impact, focusing on something unattainable – a big stretch, and focusing on rallying employees (to mention three of the four features) means being big on mission and motivation simultaneously. It is only in this way that we can get that 'Holy Grail' of engagement.

Notes

1 The MacLeod Report, David MacLeod et al., *Engaging for Success: Enhancing Performance through Employee Engagement*, Office of Public Sector Information (2009).
2 Professor Brian Cox, *The Cox Report*, HMSO (1989).
3 Bill Bonner, The Lights are Going out at GE, MoneyWeek, 2 February (2018).
4

Most organisations have espoused values and all have behavioural norms. Where there is a gap between the two, the size of the gap is reflected in the degree of distrust within the organisation; if the gap is closed, high levels of trust usually result. If an employee sees the stated values of an organisation being lived by the leadership and colleagues, a sense of trust in the organisation is more likely to be developed, and this constitutes a powerful enabler of engagement.

MacLeod Report, op. cit

5 See, for more on this: http://bit.ly/2EFwDzt.
6

Take your pick: the conquest of the Philistines by the Hebrews; the Crusades: the German invasion of Poland; 9/11. Countless wars have been fought over stories – stories of a people holding a unique covenant with God; a city standing on a rock;

a master race with a destiny to rule the world for a thousand years; the heavenly delights in store for martyrs.

Jonah Sachs, *Winning the Story Wars*, Harvard Business Review Press (2012)

7 These two examples are given in Jonah Sachs, op. cit.
8 Again, Jonah Sachs' book is a goldmine of great ideas on crafting strategic narrative. One useful distinction he makes is between Genesis – founder stories – Symbolic – meaning stories – and Documentary – action in the real world – stories. Jonah Sachs, op. cit.
9 And that is why it is important to start with motivation, not behaviours: the mistake that so many organisations make is to try to engender or create engagement by focusing on behaviours. Since behaviours and affecting them invariably involves control and manipulation this becomes self-defeating, since it disengages employees. Start with motivation, and then behaviours follow.
10 Bureau of National Affairs, cited by Dale Carnegie & Associates, ee_tips_guidebook_blue_061813_gb.
11 The seminal book on this topic, *The War for Talent*, edited Michaels, Helen Handfield-Jones, and Beth Axelrod, Harvard Business Press (2001), perhaps unsurprisingly fails to define 'talent', saying:

> A certain part of talent elude description: you simply know it when you see it. . . We can say, however, that managerial talent is some combination of a sharp strategic mind, leadership ability, emotional maturity, communications skills, the ability to attract and inspire other talented people, entrepreneurial instincts, functional skills, and the ability to deliver results.

This, of course, sounds very much like the engaging managers and visionary leaders that we have been considering in the engagement workplace!
12 Contingency plans can range from a 'soft' scheme like creating internal mentoring processes to ensure succession, or to the 'hard' key-man insurance plans whereby loss of a key employee is financially covered.
13 'Studies show that a higher score on intrinsic rewards are related to a stronger intention to remain in the organisation' – Kenneth W. Thomas, *Intrinsic Motivation at Work*, Berrett-Koehler Publishers (2009).
14 Of course, we need to be aware of the danger of presenteeism too: presenteeism is the exact opposite of engagement, for it is when employees are 'present' – there physically – but wholly disengaged with what they are doing.
15 According to Catapult in 2016 in the UK:

> Currently, UK businesses are losing 6.9 days a year per employee due to absenteeism, which is costing the British economy £100 billion … UK employees missed 131m days in total in 2014, while absenteeism is estimated to cost the average UK business £554 per employee … nearly a quarter (23%) of UK firms report 'non-genuine absence' as their top cause [of] short term absence for non-manual workers and one in three (30%) businesses also cite this as their top reason for short term absence for manual workers … Oli Johnson, co-founder of Catapult, said, The scale of the UK's absenteeism problem is simply staggering. British firms are currently losing nearly a week's worth of productivity from employees and this is having a detrimental effect on their bottom lines.
>
> http://bit.ly/2BBmuhx

16 David Bowles et al., *The High Engagement Work Culture*, Palgrave Macmillan (2012).
17 Kaisen is a Japanese word meaning 'change for the better' with an implied sense of continuous improvement. It started shortly after the end of World War 2 and revolutionised Japanese industry, leading to the creation of world-leading companies and brands, Toyota, perhaps, being the most famous.
18 There is increasing evidence that SRI (Sustainable, Responsible Investing) and ESG (Environmental, Social and Governance) committed organisations, which will tend to be the companies that promote, say, equality in the work place and human and labour rights (which promotes engagement of course) outperform companies that do not do these things. Citing research by the Boston Consulting Group, Sarah Moore says: 'Top performers in certain ESG topics had margins that were up to 12.4% higher, all things being equal, than those median performers in those topics'. MoneyWeek, Fit for the Future: how ethical investing went mainstream, 16 February 2018.
19 'The solution to the perceived conflict between financial performance and sustainable actions is to recognise that, over the long term, one is not possible without the other', Colin Melvin, MoneyWeek, 16/2/18.
20 One famous example is Terry Leahy, the ex-CEO of Tesco, who was famous for actually regularly working at the checkouts of Tesco stores: Terry Leahy chipping in at the Brent Cross Tesco checkout till! http://dailym.ai/2GNteMx. This enabled him to find out what customers really thought and wanted, and also to learn the actual issues that staff were facing. In a completely different sector, for example, education, head teachers often teach one or two periods a week precisely in order not to lose touch with what is going on in the classrooms.
21 'When Paul Allen and I started Microsoft over 30 years ago, we had big dreams about software', recalls Gates.

> We had dreams about the impact it could have. We talked about a computer on every desk and in every home. It's been amazing to see so much of that dream become a reality and touch so many lives. I never imagined what an incredible and important company would spring from those original ideas.
> *Daily Telegraph*, Claudine Beaumont, 27 June 2008,
> http://bit.ly/2t0YCVP

> However, this sense of big vision has now largely evaporated for Microsoft: commenting on Kai-Fu Lee's defection from Microsoft to Google in 2005, Richard Karlgaard observed, 'You can guess what Lee's motivation to jump ship was. At Google one works to change the world; at Microsoft one works to protect the Windows and Office profit margins. Which mission do you think high-IQ people prefer?' – *Forbes*, Talent Wars, 31 October 2005, http://bit.ly/2F4V9Hj. This only emphasises the need to remain fresh, and reminds how easy it is, once serious growth occurs, to lose sight of the original vision.

22 Jacob Morgan, *The Employee Experience Advantage*, Wiley (2017).
23 According to management consultant, Jeff Callander, 'Engagement surveys show less than 40% feel they have clarity about the business direction and their potential contribution'. Executive Learning Partnership, http://bit.ly/2Fj96ES. Of course we are not great fans of employment surveys, but even so the figure is low.

Chapter 8

Employee engagement, integrity and change

Finally, we reach the fourth enabler of employee engagement according to the MacLeod Report: integrity. And what is that? Throughout our discussion of employee engagement, we have stressed the importance of the intangibles and the invisibles in determining outcomes not just for organisations, but for individuals and teams too. Nowhere is this more apparent than in considering the question of integrity; for this too seems to be a 'fluffy', optional extra of a concept in the hard world of business or organisational success.

But before commenting on what it is, it should be clear that organisational integrity can only be a result of people integrity, and this has to start at the top. In other words, we are back to a theme, strand or topic that runs through so many of our chapters: leadership and engaging managers. Whatever the skills, knowledge, expertise and competence of these leaders, without integrity all comes to nothing. As David Brooks[1] commented: 'If you don't have some inner integrity, eventually your Watergate, your scandal, your betrayal, will happen'.

Activity 8.1

What, then, for you does integrity mean? Can you define it? And what examples for you best exemplify it in action? Which individual role models represent integrity in the past and in the modern world? Which organisations do you associate with integrity in how they operate?

According to MacLeod, integrity is when: 'Behaviour throughout the organisation is consistent with stated values, leading to trust and a sense of integrity'. This is good, although somewhat circular; and also it puts the cart before the horse: behaviour appears first, and then a sense of integrity follows. So really this is the wrong way round: integrity precedes behaviour, and behaviour follows from integrity. It is entirely possible to fake behaviour and appear to have integrity, but if one is 'faking it' in this area, one is ultimately not going to 'make it'.

What, then, is integrity? The word integrity comes from a Latin word meaning 'whole' or oneness: integrity means that a person is morally complete, unbroken, unimpaired, uncorrupted, sound, upright, honest, sincere. One could go on, but this is not a skill per se; yes, we can fake being honest, sincere, upright and so on, but if in our hearts we are not, then the circumstances will arise where we are exposed, and all comes crashing down. Shakespeare's words[2] via his character Polonius (who is in fact a pompous and crashing bore!) are often quoted in this respect: 'To thine own self be true, / And it must follow ... / Thou canst not then be false to any man', but this in our view is not enough to guarantee integrity, for it is easy enough to deceive oneself that one is following one's own 'true' self. No, in fact the reality or possibility of integrity within us seems to derive from a source external to us; it is not a subjective thing, but a way of being that arises in a conscience finely attuned to what are called the Tao, the Eightfold Path, the 10 Commandments, the Sermon on the Mount, the Super Conscious Mind, or most simply of all, God. Paradoxically, each person seems to have their own revelation about what this is, but it is never something 'post-modern', or merely subjective, or just a 'point of view'. It is like an imperative to be true to the Truth, as this comes alive in our lives.

Activity 8.2

Two questions perhaps arise from this discussion: one, how do we establish whether somebody is 'integrous'[3] or not? Two, how do we develop integrity if it is not a skill? How would you answer these two difficult questions?

Of course, to know whether somebody is 'integrous' we are beset by the ambiguity of never knowing what their actual feelings, thoughts or intentions are, because we cannot read their mind;[4] but on the other hand, what we look for is a consistency between their words and their actions, and in the case of leaders these need to be, and are, constantly scrutinised. Indeed, even our children constantly scrutinise their parents and carers, both for their internal consistency, and where there are two carers, mutual consistency: are messages from 'mum' and 'dad' saying the same thing? So the classic expression often used is relevant here: does the leader, does the engaging manager, 'walk the talk?'

In Chapter 4 we identified four criteria that demonstrate a leader – or indeed anyone – exhibiting integrity. We shall look at these four criteria shortly, but before we do we wish to return to how Motivational Maps can help here, and expand our ideas from Chapter 6 on the 360° Feedback process. Essentially, and turning this on its head, leaders can build greater trust with staff by a process of being open, and through targeted disclosure. To be clear: this is not about leaders wearing their hearts-on-their-sleeves and emotionalising their lives in order to identify more closely with those they manage, but it is important that employees know where their bosses are coming from, and nowhere more so than in the area of motivation. What does my boss actually want?

It is frequently the case in our experience that leaders and managers love to subject staff to diagnostic, psychometric and other auditing instruments, but frequently either do not do them themselves, or more likely, withhold sharing their results. This leads to Jacob Morgan's observation:[5] 'How can we expect employees to swallow that same pill when the leaders who work there won't?' Sharing one's Motivational Map results with your team is an incredible process to foster understanding, collaboration, and a renewed sense of common purpose through a shared language.

You will remember from Chapter 6 and Figure 6.5 that we asked each team member to complete a Map on an individual in their team based on what they said or did and what they knew of them. The whole process commenced electronically; however, what if we start another way – and what if we don't have access to the actual Motivational Maps online? This would effectively, then, be a group exercise, practical, physical and direct!

The first step would be to ask the team when they were gathered together for this purpose what each member thinks are their top three and lowest motivators. To do this we suggest using Figure 8.1.

Clearly, to enable the team to do this, each motivator needs to be explained separately, using the three descriptors as per Figure 8.1. So, for example, the Searcher is someone who wants or seeks meaning, making a difference, and providing worthwhile things. Once they have done this, they have the 'hang' of the process, so that they can apply it to their team members, and crucially to their leader. But at this point they do not share what they have written down.

We then move to stage two (Figure 8.2). In turn the team is then asked to predict and/or pick the top three and lowest motivations for each person in the team, including the leader. When each member of the team, including the leader, has made their prediction, they each reveal their answers. For those who may not be working in a team, then we suggest that an interesting variant of this exercise would be to think about your family, and how you would rank order their top three plus lowest motivator, and then ask them to complete their predictions: that should be fun!

Unsurprisingly, it is very rare in our experience, and as Figure 6.5 shows, for team members to be able to accurately predict not only their own, but other colleague's motivators. This is a standalone exercise, and in some ways it is not critical at this point that one actually knows the real motivators of each team member; what is important is the discussion around the issue, and in particular that the leader is open in sharing what they perceive to be their motivators, and how others see them.

Of course, there is great enrichment to this process if we do then add the actual Map findings, and this will again often be a very different result from what self or colleague predict is the case. And again, we come back the 'integrous' leader and why this is such an important activity to undertake; for who stands to lose the most by being 'wrong', by not knowing what motivates them or even their team that they are supposedly managing? Right! It's the leader who stands to lose face. In some sense they do lose face, and the leader who has to be right, who has to know everything or know more than his team, for that leader, yes, there is a palpable danger – a

RANK ORDER YOUR MOTIVATORS Description of Motivational Maps 9 motivators	Please identify top 3 motivators (1, 2 and 3) and the lowest (L)
SEARCHER (G) Seeks meaning, making a difference, providing worthwhile things.	
SPIRIT (G) Seeks freedom, independence, making own decisions.	
CREATOR (G) Seeks innovation, identification with new, expressing creative potential.	
EXPERT (A) Seeks expertise, mastery, specialization.	
BUILDER (A) Seeks money, material satisfactions, above average living standards.	
DIRECTOR (A) Seeks power, influence, control of people/resources.	
STAR (R) Seeks recognition, respect, social esteem.	
FRIEND (R) Seeks belonging, friendship, fulfilling relationships.	
DEFENDER (R) Seeks security, predictability, stability.	

Figure 8.1 Rank order your nine motivators

risk – in undertaking such an exercise. But it is precisely in moving away from such a limiting and hierarchical model of leadership that this whole employee engagement process is designed to facilitate. If one's ego is the determining factor of one's leadership style, then let's kiss employee engagement goodbye.

Activity 8.3

Review the predictions in Figure 8.3. As our focus is integrity in this chapter, pay particular attention to:

NAMES OF TEAM MEMBERS	ORDER	SELF PREDICTION	LEADER'S PREDICTION	TEAM MEMBER 1 PREDICTION	TEAM MEMBER 2 PREDICTION	TEAM MEMBER 3 PREDICTION	(OPTIONAL) ACTUAL MAP RESULT
LEADER NAME	1						
	2						
	3						
	L						
TEAM MEMBER 1	1						
	2						
	3						
	L						
TEAM MEMBER 2	1						
	2						
	3						
	L						
TEAM MEMBER 3	1						
	2						
	3						
...ETC. ADD MORE AS NECESSARY	L						

Figure 8.2 Team Map prediction blank grid

a.   How the leader, Jo, perceives their own top three and lowest motivators.
b.   How accurate are they compared with Jo's real Map result?
c.   How accurate is Team Member one, Harry, in predicting his leader's motivator?
d.   How accurate is the leader in predicting the motivators of Harry, Team Member one?
e.   What are the implications of these predictions?

Essentially, these results – and they are typical – reveal how little we really know of our own and other people's motivators. And if we if we were rewarding an individual based on what we think motivated them we might be completely wrong. One curiously odd thing (which we have noticed many times before) is that quite often lowest motivations are perceived as being in the top three by the team! So this is great awareness exercise, and not only that but sharing these predictions is an excellent way of being open and showing genuineness, for understanding what motivates the leaders is important for the employees.

If we consider the leader's self-predictions, we see that although she correctly identifies two of her motivators, the Searcher and the Builder, she completely

NAMES OF TEAM MEMBERS	ORDER	SELF PREDICTION	LEADER'S PREDICTION	TEAM MEMBER 1 PREDICTION	TEAM MEMBER 2 PREDICTION	(OPTIONAL) ACTUALMAP RESULT
LEADER NAME Jo	1	Builder		Defender		Spirit
	2	Searcher		Searcher		Searcher
	3	Star		Friend		Builder
	L	Defender		Builder		Friend
TEAM MEMBER 1 Harry	1	Director	Defender			Defender
	2	Builder	Searcher			Searcher
	3	Star	Expert			Friend
	L	Friend	Builder			Builder
TEAM MEMBER 2	1					
	2					
	3					
	L					

Figure 8.3 Team Map prediction example grid

misses her single most important motivator, the Spirit. Think about that for moment: she isn't consciously aware that the single most important satisfaction she gains from working is the need to be autonomous and independent. That is a critical omission, especially when you are leading a team, for leadership – being responsible for others – automatically implies a curtailment of one's freedom to act. Thus, being aware of this issue is vital if one is to set up a leadership style that motivates one's self as well as the team members. That said, however, we see another common phenomenon here, which is that Jo has accurately pre-dicted Harry's real motivational profile. This is the sign of a good – an engaging – manager. For what is common is the fact that oftentimes we can read other people but have a blank spot in regard to ourself.[6]

On the other hand, we find that Harry, Team Member one, has more or less completely not understood what is driving, Jo, his boss. Yes, he has got right that she wants to make a difference, the Searcher, but has entirely got wrong her competitive instincts, the Builder, and certainly missed the Spirit, the single most important drive. Indeed, if we look closely at Harry's own self-predictions we find that he is almost entirely not self-aware of what is motivating him. Two particularly interesting things are: clearly, at work he likes to project the idea that he's there for the money (Builder at number two), whereas in reality money is not that important to him; it is his lowest motivator. Furthermore, his actual Map profile is what he is projecting onto Jo, his boss: two out of his own top three, and his lowest, are what he incorrectly assesses Jo as having! This confirms what we already know: that we all have a tendency to distort reality and also to project onto it the assumption that it is like us. Put basically, if I like ice cream, everyone should like ice cream. Who couldn't like ice cream? And this, of course, is such a dangerous, even fatal, assumption. People are not like us, and on the question of what drives, what motivates them, this is especially true.

Finally, then, we need to say (and we have deliberately restricted this team to just two people because otherwise the results would take a whole chapter to analyse, but we hope the principles are clear!) that this process leads to greater understanding, empathy and sharing for the whole team. And for the leader – the engaging manager – it seems a vital methodology that will help them not only to understand what they need to do to motivate their employees, but also to demonstrate to these same employees an openness, a sharing, a genuine desire to support, that could be summed up as a major contribution towards being 'integrous'.

We now return to what we identified towards the end of Chapter 4 as being critical to empowering the employee voice, but which in fact is also crucial for the engaging manager and 'integrous' leader. Integrity cuts both ways: employees and their managers all need to practise integrity if there is going to be any chance of long-term organisational survival. But integrity must begin with the boss, since it is from the leadership that the whole quality of the culture is determined; indeed, leadership is the single most important factor determining success in almost all situations, and research by Kouzes and Posner[7] found that staff, when asked what leadership attributes they most wanted, answered competence (63%), inspiration (68%), vision (75%) and honesty (88%). Honesty – a synonym for integrity – outranked every other attribute.

The four key mind-sets we referred to in Chapter 4 were:

1. Personal responsibility
2. Avoidance of blame
3. Positive regard[8]
4. Genuineness.

And these are undoubtedly and intimately related to integrity and the practise of integrity; indeed, they could be said to be core dimensions of integrity.

Activity 8.4

Jot down two or three reasons why each of these mind-sets might be considered necessary to or demonstrative of the practice of integrity.

Perhaps the foremost rule of all life – not just organisational life – is taking personal responsibility for everything that happens to you. As Dr Norman Doidge[9] puts it: 'the foremost rule is that you must take responsibility for your own life. Period'. This taking responsibility amounts to the avoidance of three major psychological problems that beset us and damage our relationships with others, as well as being deleterious to ourselves. These three psychological problems are: blaming others (so they are responsible for difficulties), projecting our issues onto to others (so distorting reality about other people), and denial (in which we ourselves block the legitimate feedback that comes from reality).

Thus, we should be able to see how from the avoidance of 'personal responsibility' (1) we end up, as a consequence, in not 'avoiding blame' (2), which invariably means shifting it onto somebody else. That shifting it on to 'somebody else' means we are not really treating them with 'positive regard' (3), and that in turn undermines for others their sense of our 'genuineness' (4). In short, when we fail to take personal responsibility we are creating a chain that starts with lying to yourself, and then to others; so there can be no integrity in such a position.

The starting point, then, is addressing the personal responsibility issue; we have to ask how can we counter this? This is not easy, but the start of all progress has to be developing self-awareness, and from that devising a simple strategy that enables us to cope with the challenges that come our way. So, importantly, we need to understand the two vital consequences or ideas that flow from not taking personal responsibility. Firstly, if we do not take personal responsibility in our life for everything that happens to us we will, as sure as eggs are eggs, blame others; we will not be able to stop ourselves, for the central mantra of someone not taking responsibility is always, 'It's not my fault'.[10] But the second, and equally serious consequence, is that we identify ourselves as victims. We fail, but 'it's not our fault', and we are victims of circumstances; 'I could have been a contender but . . .'[11] This state of mind affects and infects our self-image and our self-esteem at a profound level, and repeated identification with it ends up creating a loser mind-set. The opposite of being a victim is being a champion, but perhaps even better, since it alliterates,[12] it's being a victor!

Activity 8.5

Are you a victim or a victor? How do you know? What evidence do you have? Since most people often see themselves as sometimes one and then the other, how can you become more consistently a victor?

When we consider the decisions we make, which lead to the choices we choose, one thing becomes abundantly apparent: either we take personal responsibility and thereby open ourselves up the possibility of learning, or we do not, and become immersed in victimhood, which invariably leads to self-recrimination and blame. The final outcomes of these vital decisions are what in old theological language might be called the choice between heaven and hell.

Being a victim – being in hell – is highly stressful because we have to keep constructing our imaginary and delusory defences that keep reality and awareness at bay; that is extremely tiring and exceedingly time consuming. Instead of becoming productive people, we trivialise ourself through the obsession with justifying our own ego's need to be right, to be important, or to be noticed. To be in heaven, on the other hand, is to be free of such constraint, and free of the stress that inevitably accumulates through self-justification; it means we can be productive and enter a newer and creative land where we can respond appropriately and positively, and without the need to react negatively.

If we look at Figure 8.4 we see clearly that victimhood leads to three levels of blame: we blame ourself, we blame others, and finally we blame circumstances. This last point of blame is often referred to colloquially as 'luck': we (or I) lost because we were 'unlucky'. It is true of course that unexpected and bad things can happen to people at any time in their lives, but it is also true that opportunities are also besieging us at all times. But sadly for the person with the negative mind-set, they cannot take advantage of these opportunities. There is an expression, sometimes attributed to the famous golfer, Gary Player, which goes: 'The harder I practise, the luckier I get', and this is the essence of taking personal responsibility; as is 'chance favours the prepared mind'.[13] Ultimately, luck has very little to do with it.

Activity 8.6

Review your own life, both at work and at home. Do you habitually blame yourself, blame others, or blame circumstances for the outcomes and condition of your life and work? Which of the three areas of blame most affects you? What do you need to do to mitigate or reduce this negativity in your life?

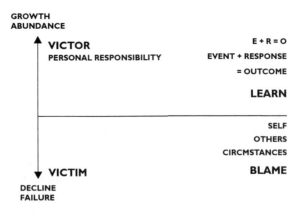

Figure 8.4 Victor or victim?

Remember, if you don't take responsibility for this area of your life, then you are devaluing your own importance to the world.

The three questions under personal responsibility in Figure 8.5 are a powerful antidote to assigning blame or becoming a victim. Practise asking them in every situation you find yourself.

With this in mind, then, we can also see that the key variable we can influence is not events – they will happen whatever we do – but our response to events. How we respond will determine the outcome and also our perception of the outcome. We need, in short, to change our thinking,[14] and the single most important idea here is the thought or question of 'what can we learn' from what happens to us? We make the distinction between a reaction – an immediate, automatic, almost automated, negative programme through which we lash out – and a response, which is a considered, responsible, judicious reply to whatever has happened, and which seeks as its primary aim to resolve, mitigate, ameliorate the problem, issue, or challenge presented to us. Reactions tend to inflame and exacerbate situations; responses tend to calm and settle them.

There is much more to say about all of this, but a pressing issue is: is there any aspect of personal responsibility, avoiding blame, showing positive regard, and being genuine that is specifically related to Mapping Motivation? Surprisingly, there is!

Why surprisingly? Because quite obviously the Maps do not in themselves represent mind-sets or integrity or other such similar intangible qualities; they describe motivation. But as we have established, it is in the 'response' to events that

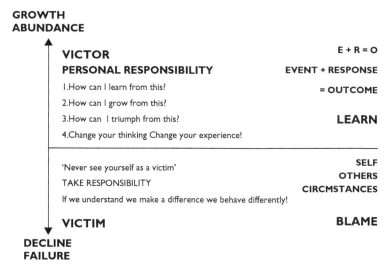

Figure 8.5 Learning or blaming?

we achieve an outcome that we either learn from, or we don't by slipping into the alternative mode of blame. This, then, gets us to one of the trickiest elements of Motivational Maps to manage: namely, 'our' response to a low motivational score. 'Our' here means: the individual's personal response (or reaction) to it, the team's response to it, and at the top of the chain of command, how the organisation views the Map scores. After all, we all want to have a highly motivated set of employees, because we know high motivation correlates with high performance, so conversely, low motivation scores are 'bad', aren't they?

It is very easy to take a judgemental view that motivationally low-scoring employees are under-performing, at fault, and bad apples who are infecting the more highly motivated staff. This can lead very easily to using Maps to 'weed' out employees who are poorly motivated, and this is wrong or misguided for two reasons. First, what it is doing is blaming others for their poor performance in the organisation – the very crime of a mind-set that we need to resist! And second, it is avoiding examining why employees, or any employee in particular, is poorly motivated. We like to say that most employees on day one of their new job are usually highly motivated; they are pleased to have the job. So what is it that leads them become demotivated over a period of time (Figure 8.6)?

Instead of blaming employees, then, we need to learn from them. There are many reasons why staff become disengaged and demotivated over time (Figure 8.7). These include, in no particular order: lack of appropriate rewards, personal and home issues, overload, lack of variety, too much change, poor communication, lack of meaning, lack of vision, motivational conflicts, personality differences, leadership

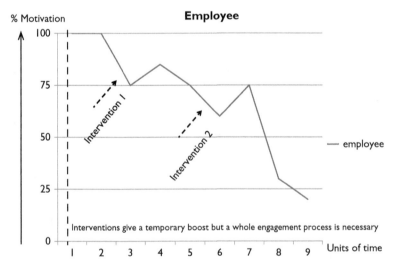

Figure 8.6 Motivation and time

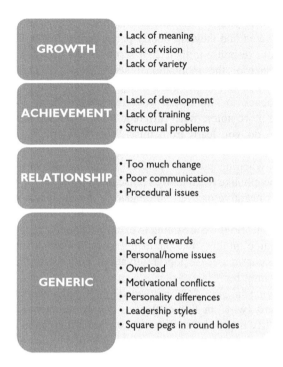

GROWTH
- Lack of meaning
- Lack of vision
- Lack of variety

ACHIEVEMENT
- Lack of development
- Lack of training
- Structural problems

RELATIONSHIP
- Too much change
- Poor communication
- Procedural issues

GENERIC
- Lack of rewards
- Personal/home issues
- Overload
- Motivational conflicts
- Personality differences
- Leadership styles
- Square pegs in round holes

Figure 8.7 Some reasons for demotivation

styles, structural problems, procedural issues, lack of development, poor training, square pegs in round holes, and so on. If we think about all these reasons – and there are more still – it might be helpful to consider them from a motivational perspective: some are quite specifically connected to the three elements of relationship, achievement and growth type motivators, whereas the others are more generic, and apply across the whole spectrum.[15]

Certainly, upon investigation – and a key word here is 'curiosity' (that is, be curious about your staff) – it may be that an employee must be let go of or moved internally, as there is simply no remedy to improve their current situation. But positive regard and genuineness dictates that our first step is to address what the issue is, and not to react with blame and punitive measures; for as with appraisals, once staff feel that the purpose is condemnatory, there can be no honest exchange of views, and the cover-up on both sides begins.

Activity 8.7

Consider or imagine that you have an employee who has just done a Motivational Map. Their motivational score is 26%: they are in the action zone of motivation. Envision two very different scenarios. Firstly, that the motivational score correlates with your assessment of their performance: in other words, they are poorly motivated and they are poorly performing. How would you feedback to him or her your response to their 26% score? Make notes on what you would say. Second scenario: the motivational score does not correlate with their performance: they have hit target, are doing extremely well in their work. How would you feedback to him or her your response to their 26% score in this situation? Make more notes. What differences are there between the two sets of feedback? What do you learn from this? What will you do about it in your practice?

Feeding back when people underperform generally is invariably an awkward task; very few people like to do it. We realise that people can be sensitive to what they perceive as negative or even unfounded criticism. If that's true for performance, then it is equally true for motivation: to be poorly motivated doesn't sound good, does it? So if we are going to exercise 'positive regard' and also to be considered 'genuine' in this situation, then we need to give it some thought.

If we take scenario one – poor motivation, poor performance – then the starting point cannot be:

'Sam, why are you only 26% motivated?' Although this seems innocuous enough, the word 'why' in this context is deeply threatening; it requires the employee to justify him or herself; it requires, too, articulation about something that we already have said is invisible, intangible and generally nebulous! Not easy, especially if we consider this may be a lower ranking operative who has just done the map for the first time.

A much better response from the engaging manager might be this:

Point one: positioning maps as non-judgemental

Sam, I want to discuss your Motivational Map with you ... First, I just need to say that all Maps are right; there are no bad Maps, they simply describe how things are in a snapshot of time. And another good thing, Sam, is that they change over time, so we are looking at your snapshot now. Whatever the result is now does not stereotype you in future.

Point two: taking responsibility and assigning no blame

To be really clear here, motivation – your motivation, Sam – I regard as my – as management's – responsibility, so wherever you are, it's up to me to help you move this forward and improve the situation.

Point three: showing positive regard

Tell me about your motivational score, Sam: is it accurate, relevant, or useful? How do you feel about it, or what can you say about it?

Note: at this point the important thing is to get the employee to talk about his or her score. In a non-threatening environment where – to use W.E. Deming's phrase[16] – fear is driven out, the employee will openly discuss the reason(s) why their motivational score is so low. That reason becomes the basis of the engaging manager's action. Notice also, the almost casual tone of the questioning: 'Tell me about ...', and not 'why'. If even that is too much, then there is the option of the closed question or questions: did you find it accurate, relevant or useful? If they answer 'yes' to 'relevant' or 'useful', then 'How exactly ...?' clearly follows on. And then 'how do you feel about ...' One can have incorrect thoughts, but we can never be wrong about how we feel; it's just how things are.

Point four: maintaining genuineness

To maintain being genuine is not, of course, a specific question; it is a consistent attitude and behaviour. If we review points one to three we see that our approach has been non-judgemental, open, flexible, concerned, curious, and decisive; and beyond the interview, it is necessary to continue being these things. And on the last word, 'decisive', that will be shown by the engaging manager taking seriously what the employee informs him or her of, and taking appropriate and prompt action on the basis of it. When people act like this they become role models[17] for everybody within an organisation, and when they become role models that then opens up the possibility of credible mentors who can support others; in short, we get to a virtuous cycle in which promoting integrity becomes everyone's concern and passion.

If we now consider the second scenario – poor motivation, high performance – we need to realise a couple of points. First, that this scenario is much rarer, and for obvious reasons: it is actually very stressful to perform at a high level and be poorly motivated. It means that the employee is operating from will-power, and not from emotional consent. This is an important issue because it also means that ultimately this position will become unsustainable: the individual will become either very stressed, or get depressed, or fall ill, or quit abruptly, or blow-up or implode in some less or more catastrophic manner. Thus, the engaging manager is not going to brush the information of the low motivational score under the carpet because 'Sam is performing all right' or 'Sam is our most highly productive member of staff', as if to say, 'so job done!' That would be a serious dereliction of the engaging manager's duty of care – of positive regard – for their employee.

On the contrary, we now need to examine what is going on with Sam just as closely and carefully as we did in scenario one. The possible difference in approach really comes at point three. Whereas in scenario one we left aside the issue of performance because it would muddy the waters of the motivational score, now, given the high performance, it would be good to introduce this factor. So

Point three (scenario two): showing positive regard

I am really curious, Sam, can you explain something to me?
PAUSE/REPLY
    You are so on top of your role, and are such a high performing member of staff, I don't understand why your motivational score of 26% is as it is? Can you help me? How has that come about?

Here we have the opportunity to reinforce their high performance and so value to the organisation; that's easy to do, as it sounds like praise. But the important thing is to press ahead and discover why the motivational score is low. Invariably, when we have done this, the reasons are always significant: often it is personal, either in the home or to do with conflict with another colleague, and sometimes it is shocking. On one occasion, for example, we discovered using this methodology that the highest performing sales person in the UK, in a substantial, internationally-operating SME (small- or medium-sized enterprise), actually hated their job (and its relentless pressure) but had a five-year plan (and they were now near the end of year two) in which the individual would make enough money to be able to retire – and give it all up. This 'shocked' senior management who hadn't even dreamed that their star performer was even remotely unhappy; the sales person conceded they appeared upbeat and positive because they knew that was what a successful sales person had to be. But inside their psyche, all was very different! How valuable, then, is knowing this information? First, they could begin to redress some issues about the work that perhaps might make it less onerous for their 'star'; and second they now could succession plan what they might need to do should the sales person resign at any point.

    And this is where the Maps are helpful yet again. For what we are talking about in essence is change: people come and go, but people are the life blood of an organisation; they are the organisation's major asset. Their knowledge, their skills, their experience, their contacts, their creativity – to mention just five aspects of their contributions – are vital. We need to be able to cope with and adapt to change, especially change as something that specifically affects employees, including their retention.

    Typically, the difference in performance terms between well-led (by engaging managers) and poorly-led employees is shown in Figure 8.8. The huge dip in performance might be the simple loss of a key person, and so the new inductee will take a while before they get up to speed, or it might be simply a failure to address other issues[18] that explain why the organisation is failing. Whatever the reason, what we want to address is how we reverse the losses that are accruing to us. This is complex, but one issue here relevant to Maps is that of change and its twin sibling, risk. Over times things change,[19] and we can react or we can respond to that. But if we respond we will be well aware that all change involves risk. And, despite its ubiquity, 'enormous energy goes into resisting change'.[20]

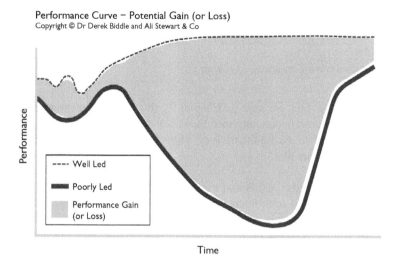

Performance Curve – Potential Gain (or Loss)
Copyright © Dr Derek Biddle and Ali Stewart & Co

Figure 8.8 Leading change and transition

Source: With permission from Dr Derek Biddle and Ali Stewart, Liberating Leadership, Rethink Press Ltd (2015), https://bit.ly/2HBMYGM.

But how much energy, exactly? How big is the task ahead of us if we want to effect change? Have we adequately estimated the scale of the difficulty ahead, particularly as it appertains to keeping the staff motivated and engaged – which ultimately means, retained?

Obviously, this is a highly complex issue, but one formula together with one tool that we have found useful in getting a preliminary handle on what needs to be done are the overcoming resistance to change formula and the Motivational Map change index score.

The overcoming resistance to change formula[21] that we think manageable is shown in Figure 8.9.

For change to be successful there has to be a compelling vision – a leadership issue – plus sufficient resources to deliver on that vision. The necessary resources, of course, will be identified as the action plan takes shape. But the fascinating and unexpected ingredient in this formula, the one we want to focus on now, is 'dissatisfaction with the status quo'! We will comment on this shortly, but the combination of V, R and DwSQ must be greater than the cost of the change if change is to be successful.

What, then, is this dissatisfaction with the status quo? It means that all staff, including management and senior management, must be unhappy with the way things are now,[22] with the current state of affairs as it were. But given that management mostly sees its role as 'improving' things, the real issue is staff themselves being unhappy with the current situation or state of things. We

Figure 8.9 Overcoming resistance to change

already know, in fact we saw in Chapter 1, that most employees don't like change; it introduces uncertainty into their lives and their work.

Employees will be asking themselves, and sometimes each other formally and informally, questions like:

1. Will my knowledge, skills and expertise still be of value?
2. How motivated or committed will I be to perform if this change takes place?
3. Will my department or team gain or lose status or power in the change?
4. What will the consequences, perceived or real, be of complying or resisting?
5. How much do I trust my leader and/or the organisation to look after me?
6. How much support will there be from the organisation for this change?
7. How do I really feel about this? Do I feel good?
8. What are the consequences of success or failure?

Thus, as Andrew Leigh[23] succinctly expressed it: 'The status quo is thus the pivot on which resistance revolves'. If we, as employers, could answer these eight questions satisfactorily, then we would be a long way on the road to having an engaged workforce. But here's the thing from the Mapping Motivation point of view: we can know just how much resistance to change employees are likely to have from the Team (or Organisational) Motivational Map. Within the Map there is something called the change index score. To be clear: the change index score does not tell you what to do; what it does do is indicate the level of difficulty one might have in effecting change, and so enable one to predict more accurately in advance the level of resourcing that the organisation is going to need to make this change work.

The change index looks that shown in Figure 8.10 and is found on page 17[24] of any Team Motivational Map.

Another way of putting this is: how risk-friendly or risk-averse are the team/ organisation?

One further point to note is that teams which are change-friendly/risk-friendly tend to move faster than teams that are change-resistant/risk-averse, which tend to move at a slower pace. The reason is clear: change-friendly teams tend to seek effectiveness whereas change-resistant teams tend to seek efficiency. Again, neither is better or worse, but the context is decisive in deciding what kind of team or organisational focus we need in a given situation.

There are four quadrants of change.

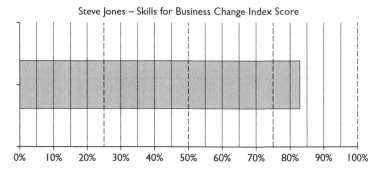

Steve Jones – Skills for Business Change Index Score

0%   10%   20%   30%   40%   50%   60%   70%   80%   90%   100%

Your team has a change index score of 83% meaning that this team has a very positive attitude to change and is very risk friendly. They will tend to want to move at a very fast pace with a focus on effectiveness and outcomes. People and things need to 'work' – result are paramount.

Figure 8.10 Change index score example

Quadrant 1 – above 75%, which reflects a very positive attitude to change, very risk friendly. They will tend to want to move at a very fast pace with a focus on effectiveness and outcomes. People and things need to 'work' – results are paramount.

Quadrant 2 – above 50%, which reflects a positive attitude to change, risk friendly. They will tend to want to move at a fast pace with a focus on effectiveness and outcomes. Systems and things need to 'work' – results are important.

Quadrant 3 – above 25%, which reflects a conservative attitude to change and is risk averse. They will tend to want to move at a quite slow pace with a focus on efficiency and care. Systems and things need to be 'right' – accuracy is important.

Quadrant 4 – above 0%, which reflects a deeply conservative attitude to change and is very risk averse. They will tend to want to move at a very slow pace with a focus on efficiency and detail. People and things need to be 'right' – accuracy is paramount.

If we consider these quadrants and think about the resources we need to bring to bear to effect change, then it should be clear that the lower the score, especially below the 50% mark, the more resources are needed to persuade the staff to go along with the changes and remain engaged.

There are nine types of resources, but notice that they fall into three categories: tangibles, intangibles and people development. In terms of levels of difficulty, providing a tangible –money, for example – is relatively easy; providing an intangible – such as time – is more complex, and ensuring that people are 'developed' sufficiently – for example, having the right attitude – is the most difficult of all – and what this book is about![25]

		CHANGE INDEX QUADRANTS			
		Q1 >75%	Q2 >50%	Q3 >25%	Q4 >0%
MONEY Tangible	How much: From where:				
TIME Intangible	When: How much:				
EQUIPMENT Tangible	What: Where from:				
PEOPLE SKILLS People development	Which: Level:				
KNOWLEDGE Intangible	What: Level:				
RIGHT ATTITUDE People development	Approach: Motivation:				
INFORMATION Intangible	What: Format:				
SPACE/ENVIRONMENT Tangible	Where: Quality:				
AGREE CO-OPERATION People development	Who: When:				

Figure 8.11 The nine resources of change

Activity 8.8

Keeping the above in mind and that there are no simple answers to these questions, review Figure 8.11. Study the nine types of resources that typically are utilised by teams and organisations. Choose any change initiative[26] you know or are considering implementing yourself. Then consider the scenario of quadrant one where your employees are high risk/high change types: in other words, there will be a preponderance of Searchers, Spirits and Creators in their profiles. Their dissatisfaction with the status quo stems from the fact that the team or organisation is less than ideal in its current configuration, but they *want* change. What kind of resources, and at what quantity, is likely to be necessary to get their buy-in? Now consider quadrant four. Here we have employees who are high risk/high change averse. Typically, they will have a preponderance of Defender, Friend and Star motivators in their profiles. Their dissatisfaction with the status quo stems from the fact that at least things are working as they are, so if it ain't broke, why fix it? They do *not* want change per se. What kind of resources, and at what quantity, is likely to be necessary to get their buy-in?

We hope that reviewing these ideas can help any team or organisation avoid the pitfall of underestimating what is required in any change programme involving employees. They help provide a level of detail beyond the big picture or vision that activates change, and enable us to fully scope what is necessary when we think of our employees.

Notes

1 David Brooks, *The Road to Character*, Random House (2015).
2 Shakespeare, Hamlet act 1, scene 3, 78–82.
3 We have put this word in single inverted commas because there is some query as to whether the adjective exists as distinct from the noun, integrity. The Oxford English Dictionary cites its use as far back as 1657 by William Morice, but it is rare: see http://bit.ly/2oXDr1F.
4 Which is why, of course, in Chapter 5 and our account of using Maps for recruitment, we show how Map-specific questions can get to the underlying 'truth' of an employee's or a hire's true motivation.
5 Jacob Morgan, *The Employee Experience Advantage*, Wiley (2017).
6 An interesting model for this is the Johari Window. For more on Johari see James Sale, *Mapping Motivation*, Routledge (2016), Chapter 3.
7 James Kouzes and Barry Posner, *The Leadership Challenge*, Wiley (2003).
8 Positive regard and genuineness are identified specifically by Ali Stewart in her book, *Insights into Liberating Leadership*, Rethink Press (2015): 'if you don't have the right underlying mind-set, if you are acting without Positive Regard and Genuineness, there is nothing to anchor the spokes and at some point the wheel will collapse'. Positive regard means having respect for the other person as an individual and a positive belief in them as a person; genuineness means you are able to express your own feelings and tell the truth about your reactions to the other person's behaviour. It means being direct, open and honest with the other person.

9   Cited in the foreword to Professor Jordan B. Peterson's brilliant book, *12 Rules for Life*, Allen Lane (2018).

10 Of course, this is not to deny the fact that sometimes it genuinely is not your/my fault; or to deny that some people even from birth are dealt a particularly hard or brutal hand (and others, to switch metaphors, are born with a 'silver spoon in their mouth'). But to use the card analogy, the key thing is not to spend one's life blaming one's parents or teachers or others for all they failed to do for you – the bad hand you have been dealt – but to play the cards you have got as dextrously and as well as possible. Weak hands, with persistence and ingenuity, can often defeat much stronger ones. Poker, as a particular card game, is a great example of this: the hand itself is often subsidiary to how it is played.

11 Famously, Marlon Brandon as Terry Malloy in the film, *On the Waterfront* (1954), said: 'You don't understand! I coulda had class. I coulda been a contender. I could've been somebody, instead of . . .' This is classic victim speak.

12 Punning, rhyming and alliterating: three compulsive vices – and joys – of the English language!

13 The actual quotation is 'Chance favours only the prepared mind' from Louis Pasteur.

14 For much more on 'changing our thinking' through coaching, see James Sale and Bevis Moynan, *Mapping Motivation for Coaching*, Routledge (2018).

15 The importance of showing this list in this way is to once again demonstrate just how many key motivational issues are directly correlated with the Maps' typology. Yes, some issues – like for example square pegs in round holes – do not seem directly connected, although they may be on deeper examination, but others – like, for example, lack of meaning – are absolutely at the roots of motivation: in this case, of course, the Searcher motivator

16 Rafael Aguayo, *Dr Deming: The Man Who Taught the Japanese about Quality*, Mercury Business Books (1991)

17 The importance of role models cannot be overstated. We all need them, and they feed our 'ideal self' – that part of our self-concept which longs to become more than it is.

18 At least five reasons, which are: the requirements aren't clear; requirements aren't taken seriously by management and staff; requirements aren't communicated; the process isn't capable of actually being done; people aren't trained sufficiently. If there is a problem, it will one or more of these – and most frequently the first reason: that the requirements be clear. T. Knoster et al., *Restructuring for Caring and Effective Education*, Brookes Publishing Co. (1999) also included skills and incentives in their list but omitted dissatisfaction with the status quo, which we see as central.

19 Again, five powerful reasons why organisationally things change are: PEST (Political, Economic, Social and Technological developments), competition, supplier/customer needs, internal forces or, quite simply, our self – we change.

20 Andrew Leigh, *Effective Change*, IPM (1988).

21 There are various iterations of this formula, depending on the expert consulted. One factor we are omitting here but which is often included is: action steps or action plan.

22 This seems highly counterintuitive when we consider that we are trying to get staff to become 'engaged', which is presumably a happier state to be in! But being engaged and simultaneously dissatisfied with the way things are is not an incompatible state of being. As a parent, for example, we may be totally engaged in bringing up our children, but at a certain point in their development be unhappy with where they are and seek to improve the situation.

23 Andrew Leigh, op. cit.
24 And page 21 of The Organisational Motivational Map.
25 A lot more detail on these issues of change will be available in the forthcoming book, James Sale, *Mapping Motivation for Strategy and Change*, Routledge (2020).
26 This really could be anything, but to take some typical examples: re-structuring the organisation, changing the salary/commission basis, re-locating, implementing new IT hardware/software/systems, responding to market changes or new competition, and so on.

Chapter 9

Three case studies

FGH, Inspire Professional Services, Aish Technologies

We have now reached the point where we need to pull together some of our ideas and see how they manifest themselves through various case studies.[1] Also, we need to share with you the process that we use to draw together the various strands we have discussed and uncovered in this book. For let's be clear: this is not a simple 'thing' to implement. Engagement is fraught with ambiguity and difficulty because people are ambiguous and difficult; and this observation is not confined to just the employees. As it should be manifest from so many examples in this work, managers and leaders too can be difficult and ambiguous, and if they are this will not facilitate staff engagement. People want communication that is clear, explicit and consistent.

What, then, might be the steps that we address in a programme to develop greater employee engagement? We think there are four key steps.

Step 1 actually does start with motivation. We need to understand what it really is – energy – and how too it is correlated with performance and productivity at both an individual and team level. In the Introduction and Chapter 1 we looked at various facets of this, but especially how Motivational Maps provides exactly the right language and metrics to be able to really get a grip on what is really happening with the people (and how they feel) in your organisation.

Step 2 is about focusing on the 'engaging manager' as MacLeod calls it, or the 'high performing manager' as Goffee and Hunt call it, or 'visible, empowering leadership', or simply 'leadership'.[2] This is a vital thread running through the whole book, for the leader has to be actively present to employees and teams, as well as communicating effectively, creating a strategic narrative, and being 'integrous'. These are facets and dimensions of truly engaging leadership that we explore throughout the various chapters.

Step 3 concerns specific skills set the leader needs: coaching skills possibly being a summary of some of the specifics we have itemised. We have tried not to repeat all the insights and ideas from our earlier book, *Mapping Motivation for Coaching*,[3] but have included some key pointers and practical applications of effective coaching, especially on feeding back Map results, establishing core values, and developing core skills.

Step 4 where, finally, we have to communicate effectively. This is part process – the HOW we do it, and so we have reviewed techniques and ideas such as VAK AD. And it is also part content: what actually is the message? Nowhere is this more important than in the strategic narrative that employees need to understand, grasp and embrace. But, also, it is both process and content simultaneously, for when we consider values it is not enough to state them (the content), but we have to demonstrate or live them (the process).

With the foregoing in mind each organisation needs to address the issues resulting from their own audit, and devise a programme that works for them, given where they are. It is impossible for one size to fit all, but it is important to stress that running and embedding an engagement programme is not the same thing as simply putting on training to upskill managers and employees. We see from Step 3 that we do need to upskill people, but this is only part of a wider cultural change. Step 5 (which is to re-visit Step 1, see Figure 9.1), after Step 4 is completed, is the ongoing re-Mapping of staff to see how things have changed as a result of the initial intervention, and this may be easier to see if we actually create a simplified visual of the cycle, as shown in Figure 9.1.

As we will see, if we break it down and follow our own step-by-step cycle, then typically we have a programme that runs over a year and takes up to 12

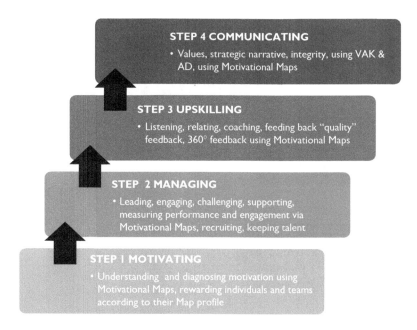

Figure 9.1 Four steps to employee engagement

days to deliver, which spreads out the required commitment of the organisation to one day a month: see Figures 9.2 and 9.4 for how this might look.

What results can we expect from such programme? Here are three short case studies outlining some perceptions of the engagement process, and what happened.

Case study 1: FGH (Financial Consultancy)

Who are FGH?[4]

FGH is a small owner-operated business providing financial and wealth management services, with aspirations to grow headcount and revenue. Historical issues included low morale, an inability to attract and retain talent, and cliques and selfish employees, with the added downside of good staff being poached by competitors. The business was underperforming in both sales and business development. Revenues had been acceptable, but the company had always struggled to retain staff. Andrew Shaw was tasked with growing the business headcount, gross revenues and profitability. He knew people were the key ...

So, within six months, the company grew from ten to 20 people. As it hit 20 staff, retention became a bigger challenge, and keeping staff levels at that number consistently was nigh on impossible. Team managers were spending

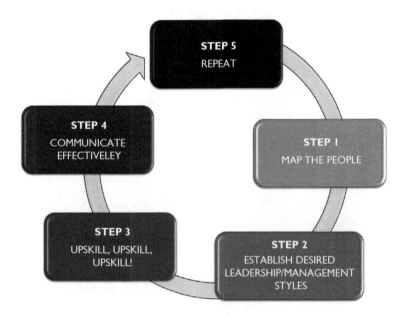

Figure 9.2 Employee engagement action cycle

	CEO	Sales Director	HR Director	Top Seller
Their MAP Profile	SPIRIT SEARCHER FRIEND	STAR BUILDER DIRECTOR	DEFENDER CREATOR FRIEND	STAR BUILDER EXPERT
What they believed was wrong	Too many selfish people and cliques.	No investment in biz. Weak biz dev team.	Poisonous atmosphere. No policies.	Not enough Leads. No training. Too much time wasted.
What they wanted to achieve	A company everyone was proud to work in and revered in the industry.	A team of decent people to manage that can hit quote.	A stable team of nice people were people enjoy being at work and don't leave.	More commission To be seen as the best in the industry.
Quantifying results wanted	Improve morale. Hire great people. Manage out bad apples.	Better sales staff. Reward based on team performance.	Reduce turn-over. Hire better people.	More money. More recognition. More opportunity.
How we achieved it using maps	Managed people as individuals. Communicated results and news across company. Did team activities (formal and informal).	Invested in hiring good people. Made commissions more meritocratic. Introduced stretch targets. Fired bad performers.	Created Job Specs. Defined hiring process. Put HR policies in place. Introduced staff suggestion box.	Invested in Lead Generation. Included him in hiring decisions. Got press attention for him/company.

Figure 9.3 Map Profile Analysis of key personnel at FGH

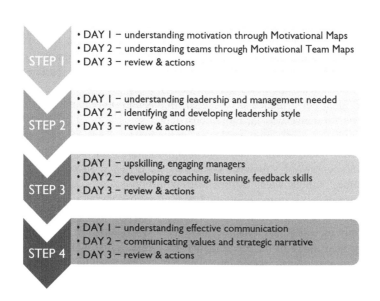

STEP 1
- DAY 1 – understanding motivation through Motivational Maps
- DAY 2 – understanding teams through Motivational Team Maps
- DAY 3 – review & actions

STEP 2
- DAY 1 – understanding leadership and management needed
- DAY 2 – identifying and developing leadership style
- DAY 3 – review & actions

STEP 3
- DAY 1 – upskilling, engaging managers
- DAY 2 – developing coaching, listening, feedback skills
- DAY 3 – review & actions

STEP 4
- DAY 1 – understanding effective communication
- DAY 2 – communicating values and strategic narrative
- DAY 3 – review & actions

Figure 9.4 Employee programme for leaders and managers

too much time people managing and interviewing. Stability and efficiency were desperately needed. Juggling the hiring and training of management, as well as driving the top line performance, was a huge challenge, and the leadership team was stretched.

Why Motivational Maps?

Fortunately, Andrew Shaw was introduced[5] to Motivational Maps as a potential solution to their problems. He saw some obvious benefits of Mapping the teams, but some vitally important benefits, not envisaged initially, became evident after commitment to using Motivational Mapping as a foundation for their people strategy.

They mapped everyone in the company, alongside targeted people management, and the results are explained below.

What happened when we used the Motivational Maps?

After the teams were mapped, the analysis enabled management to put plans in place and high impact results materialised almost immediately:

1. Staff retention recovered from an annual turnover of 100% to less than 10%! Plus, the company realised that the Maps were predictive, and that they knew which employees were thinking of leaving long before they did, and so were able to manage it proactively. Over the next two years no single staff member who was mission-critical was lost.
2. The hiring process became significantly more efficient. Candidates were mapped, and the profiles were used as the focus of the first interviews, saving countless hours of management time. Plus, the company was also able to identify any potential good or bad team fits, and possible conflicts with other team members at a very early stage.
3. Individual performance skyrocketed. Inputs and outputs not only improved but performance was far more consistent.
4. Individuals were motivated (as individuals). The Motivational Maps enabled management to see who was motivated by what. This meant some awesome reward structures could be put in place specific to each team member: things such as time off, mini-bonuses, recognition, leadership opportunities, learning opportunities (and more) cost us very little in dollar terms but was priceless in motivating everyone going from day to day. Simply put, they had a happier more energetic team. The Map reports even suggested many of the rewards that fitted each individual.
5. Management performance improved drastically. Specifically, managers had more time to focus on the sales part of their role and spent less time hiring and managing under-par performance. Also, inexperienced managers found the step-up to leadership less overwhelming; they were able to delegate

tasks to team members who wanted some level of leadership, but didn't want a management career path. This proved a huge hidden benefit for the individuals and the managers.

6. Personal development and career planning became a focus for the business and having the ability to identify potential and aspiring leaders early became a vital component of their longer-term continuity plan. They were able to plan and work towards promotions (to senior sales and sales manager roles) and even successfully moved staff into non-sales departments of the business rather than lose them. Almost as key, they knew who was not motivated by management and let them focus on sales; this could not have been executed without the Maps.

The business grew from six people to 35 people across four different teams, adding an extra 25 sales/business developers.

How did people react to the Motivational Maps? What was the impact of the Maps?

In a nutshell the whole growth structure of the company was built around the Motivational Map results. Maps laid the foundation, but as a business they were committed to building on that and they saw positive results in every area. It was hard work but well worth it. They concluded that such exponential successful growth would not have been possible without the use of Motivational Maps. They had a happier, more productive set of individuals. They had more focused and less stressed managers; the teams were more united and the camaraderie across the whole company was sensational. They slashed recruitment spend (dollars and time) and grew their leaders organically, saving hundreds of thousands on expensive senior-level hire. Implementing Motivational Maps changed the very fabric of their company.

What changes through Motivational Maps did we find?

Sales and business development:

- Top line sales performance went up by 15% within two months.
- 85% of Business development managers hit their KPI/quota (up from <40%).
- Overall improved results and consistency.

Management and leadership:

- Team leaders spent eight fewer hours per week in 1-on-1 meetings.
- Monthly and quarterly reviews were more effective and efficient.
- Short- and long-term reward structures were tailored to the individuals.
- Career paths were defined for and by individuals.

People agenda:

- The company retained one excellent employee by changing their role (to research from sales).
- Staff turnover was reduced to less than 10% (from >100%).
- People approached the business to join them.
- Drastically reduced recruiting costs (fees and time).

Overall change:

- People were happier at work and productivity went up across the company.
- The company was talked about (in positive terms) across the industry.
- The company growth led to stability.

The results of using Motivational Maps to create the engaged, loyal, committed and creative work force speak for themselves. Figure 9.3 shows in more detail some of the exact features of using Maps. Notice how the focus is not on financial metrics per se, although going through this process is exactly what the Map intervention is going to affect. But small things to spot might be: the dominance of the Star motivator in both the sales director's and top seller's profile. What would be the effect of this be? It would be to want to be in a company of high reputational standing; see how the top seller is going to be further motivated by a. including them in 'hiring decisions' (so must be a VIP, then) and b. getting 'press attention' for not only the company but for his own contribution.

Second, see how the HR director has Defender top in their profile. What will this drive? If they are allowed their way – which they were – it will drive stability, the very thing the company needs.

Third, notice too how the CEO and HR director share the Friend motivator. It will drive morale, belonging, and being part of a wider community; it will also act as a brake on too much overt sales competitiveness (Star and Builder), which can undermine cohesion.

Finally, also observe that within these four senior staff members' top three motivators, all nine motivators are expressed. This is not a requirement for each and every organisation; it can lead to a lack of focus. But in this instance the motivational diversity works for the company. The Expert, for example, only appears once, but it is the top seller who wants new learning and expertise; indeed, has complained about the lack of it. This person is crucial, and clearly the company is going to want more people in sales just like their top seller. Thus, satisfying the Expert motivator is not something they contemplate for just one person; it too needs to be core if they are going to be, as the top seller wants, 'the best in the industry'.

The Maps, therefore, are giving massive clues as to what to do, alongside informing the company what it is that their own people truly want. This is a powerful mix.

Case study 2: Inspire Professional Services (IPS)

Who are IPS?

In 2004, Warren Munson, the founder of IPS, left his tax-focused position at a major national firm, noticing an opportunity in the market for a tax and business advisory firm focused on entrepreneurs. Since then he has built a loyal team of directors and employees who support over five hundred entrepreneurs throughout the various stages of their business journey. Since 2010, IPS have won numerous business awards and have doubled in size, expanding their client base within the south west region of the UK.

Why Motivational Maps?

IPS started to look at employee engagement just before their 10th anniversary in 2014. The company had experienced rapid growth, but were in danger of losing sight of their core mission 'to enable ambitious and driven entrepreneurs to succeed'. The business was beginning to feel like a big firm, similar to the one that Warren Munson had left behind all those years ago!

Keen to make sure that IPS didn't fall into the trap of becoming yet another big accountancy firm, Warren decided to focus on employee engagement as the key differential that could make and sustain the difference he wanted; furthermore, he had heard of Motivational Maps and of its expert practitioner, Steve Jones. Steve Jones's business, Skills for Business Training Ltd., specialised in applying staff motivation to the whole engagement issue. But what Warren especially liked was the fact that Steve Jones did not pretend that there was some quick fix available: to attain employee engagement meant undertaking a rigorous and prolonged programme of activities. So Warren clearly understood and recognised – as did IPS – that the company needed to change and get back to its roots and core purpose.

Employee engagement would enable IPS to re-engage with its core essence, spirit and beliefs.

What did IPS do with the Motivational Maps?

Central to the work Steve Jones undertook with the leadership team of IPS and its employees was the use of Motivational Maps. There was an appetite to truly engage and understand the individuals and teams within the business, and to create a motivational, goal-driven organisation aligned through a common cause.

Along with many of the other concepts and ideas in this book, the use of Motivational Maps became instrumental in achieving this objective. The actual programme followed the steps outlined in Figures 9.1 and 9.2. But the programme itself looked like Figure 9.4

A couple of points to notice about this programme. First, that it is a year long, but it actually requires only one day a month's commitment, so it is spread out. In other words, it is designed to be manageable. We all recognise that it is

Figure 9.5 Inspire Professional Services' engaged employees

easy to become preoccupied with developmental projects and lose sight of the number one issue: clients and prospects. Second, because it is spread out, the intention is to prevent overload with the staff. There are many three, four or five consecutive day courses that are great in their way, but which can be over intensive. This spacing out of the training and analysis is to allow the learning to sink in at a deeper level; to be embedded. Third, it is 12 days spread over a year, but there is also a great deal of flexibility here: it does not have to be exactly *this* – or exactly *that*. The client can opt in or out of the modules as necessary. And by 'as necessary' we mean that each organisation is different. Whereas Step 1 – the Map audit – is crucial and necessary, it may be that, for example, certain parts of Step 3 or Step 4, upskilling or communicating, are not required because the managers are already strong in a certain area. For example, they may already be very good at giving feedback, so this element of the programme can be shortened. Equally, other modules may be needed and added. Finally, notice how this programme targets the leaders and managers, and day three on each of the four steps is about 'review and actions'. One central aspect of the 'actions' will always be what the managers then do with their learning, and how they share it with their employees; what is sometimes called 'cascading down'.

How did people react to the Motivational Maps?

Warren's own comment is:

> The employee engagement process that we undertook with Steve and the fundamental use of Motivational Maps in our business has been transformational to our whole approach with all members of the team. A really powerful process that has enabled us to grow the business while staying true to our core essence spirit and beliefs.
>
> Warren Munson

What about the employees? Three comments are indicative:

> It helped me understand and reinforce my own motivators, and it is good to see them in black and white. The maps are a very useful tool to help with my management of the team as they are all very different. Understanding what motivates each individual team member really helped me and I adapted my management style as a result. It is an invaluable tool to understand my team better
>
> Anne Beashel, Senior Tax Manager

> At first I was sceptical when Motivational Maps were first introduced into the business, however the results continue to be unerringly accurate and continually reflect the position you find yourself in when undergoing the process. They form such an important part of the staff development process, as they really help to clarify an individual's needs, motivators and goals, which Inspire can then focus on to ensure continued employee well-being and happiness.
>
> James Barter, Tax Manager

> At Inspire we have spent a lot of time developing our annual appraisal process. When we introduced Motivational Maps the team found using them very interesting and informative, certainly a useful tool for their development and progression.
>
> Bev Cattano, Senior Manager – Support Services

If accountants (we suggest without any disrespect, but they are number-orientated!) find the Maps accurate, useful and relevant, then we would argue any business or organisation can!

What was the impact of the maps?

IPS were able to reconnect with their core spirit, essence and beliefs and continue to grow and win awards. The business is now thriving more than ever with a workforce that are fully engaged and behind the business. And this business, as Warren Munson observed, has to be outstanding: 'Because we work with truly exceptional entrepreneurs, it's important we're constantly at the top of our game.' The employee engagement process, then, is very much alive and underpinned by the use of Motivational Maps in all areas of the business.

As Debbie Cohen, an HR consultant involved in the process[6] observed:

> As an HR professional I have seen numerous tools used within businesses to gauge employee motivation and engagement, Motivational Maps is one of these tools and it adds huge value within a business if it is used in the right way. About four years ago we reviewed our appraisal process and as

part of this we decided to take the Motivational Maps and link the process with the appraisal process. In doing this we aligned the Motivational Maps with the appraisals and added some specific questions regarding motivation within the appraisal form to allow a discussion to take place at the appraisal meeting. This gave us the framework to use the data that Motivational Maps gives us on each employee, but also enables each employee to go through the information in context with their manager. The whole process has been really positive and makes the appraisal process a positive experience for all involved.

Debbie Cohen, HR Consultant

This has led to some important recognition in terms of eminent national awards. As a role model and mentor himself, Warren Munson achieved the Business Leader of the Year award at the 2017 Dorset Business Awards. Regarded as one of Dorset Business Awards' highest accolades, the Business Leader of the Year award recognises Warren's innovation and leadership within his field, which has seen him develop a pioneering brand and launch unique entrepreneurial events.

Further, in both 2016 and 2017, IPS were crowned Independent Firm of the Year for the South West and Wales by the British Accountancy Awards, the industry's most esteemed accolade. This prestigious title is awarded to a firm with a turnover of up to £3m, who are able to demonstrate how they've added significant value to their clients and across all service areas.

Then in 2016, in The Accountancy Age Best Employer Survey, IPS scooped a top place in the Accountancy Age Best Employer award, confirming them as one of the UK's best places to work. And even more impressively, in 2017 IPS were awarded Company Star of the Year by the Rock Star Awards. This prestigious title is awarded to a firm with fewer than 50 employees, who are able to demonstrate they are hiring, training and nurturing young people.

Clearly, all this recognition was possible because of Warren's vision and determination to create a workforce with a difference – an engaged workforce, one powered by Motivational Maps, the right mind-set, and some of the tools and techniques outlined in this book. It shows how far a business can evolve, and is a far cry from the dark days of their ninth year when Warren had questioned where his business was heading.

What next?

This has all led to some serious innovation: IPS being able to support the local community and entrepreneurs. IPS now annually run an entrepreneurs' conference for over 250 entrepreneurs at the famous BIC in Bournemouth, where the successes and challenges of entrepreneurs are openly shared. In full support of their pledge 'to enable ambitious and driven entrepreneurs to succeed', IPS are excited about embarking on the next phase of their journey: their very own coaching programme for entrepreneurs – 'The Complete Entrepreneur'. The coaching programme is based on the IPS journey and those of its clients, and is outlined and captured in Warren Munson's supporting book, *The Complete Entrepreneur*, to be published in 2018.

Case study 3: Aish Technologies

Who are Aish Technologies?

Aish Technologies is a systems design and manufacturing company that specialises in the protection of electronic equipment in harsh environments. The company has a history that extends back over 100 years, and has an enviable pedigree in the supply of rugged technology across the world.

The company is based in Poole, England, in a purpose-built facility that allows the company's full range of design disciplines and advanced manufacturing techniques to be carried out on one site. Although Aish Technologies has in-depth expertise that can be applied in any number of specialist areas, the company is renowned for the development and manufacture of innovative, purpose built, rugged multi-function consoles, electronic cabinets, racks and enclosures, flat panel displays and Impressed Current Cathodic Protection (ICCP) systems. The development of these successful products has given them the expertise and knowledge to provide a service to their customers in the design, development and manufacture of a wide range of military and commercial hardware.

Why Motivational Maps?

Because Aish had grown, and through its excellent, advanced manufacturing facility aquired major customers such as BAE Systems, NGSM, Thales and SEA, it had run into a familiar problem: employee engagement, or the lack thereof. In 2015 both the MD, Lloyd Bates, and the then head of HR, Dorothy Westerman, realised that growing from 100 to 240 staff had meant that along the way the levels of engagement had slipped, and that the culture that had emerged needed challenging and changing.

If they were to maintain their position as a world-class technology company, management recognised that it needed to be committed to supporting and developing all its employees. But how? At this point they heard at a business network meeting Steve Jones talk about Motivational Maps and its impact on employee engagement, so they invited him in.

They wanted to re-capture the energy, excitement and engagement they had when there were only 100 staff, but there was a further disconnect that the business had to acknowledge and deal with: this had been brought about by the dichotomy between the old and the new, it being a second-generation business, with the previous owner, Lloyd's father, having recently retired. Clearly, this had 'factional' implications with old-guard and new-guard tending to compete rather than work together for the common good.

What did they do with the Motivational Maps?

Steve Jones proposed a year-long programme whereby the senior management team and the board met with Steve two days per month,[7] sometimes together, sometimes separately, to explore and implement an employee engagement programme.

The programme was designed to be bespoke, intuitive. And to centre around the needs of the organisation, and to be inclusive of Lloyd and Dorothy's thoughts and insights. The goal was to unite the leadership team and the board behind a common goal of employee engagement to ensure that the success of the organisation was brought about by the people it employed, harnessing their full potential and capabilities towards a common cause.

Given this design, the programme started with what Steve Jones calls a 'fact find': where are we now? What does 'good' or 'excellent' look like? Is everyone on board, as this is not just another HR issue, but it is a strategic choice. This last point, of course, 'is everyone on board ... for what is in effect a strategic choice' immediately means we need to use the Maps to audit all the employees.

How did people react to the Motivational Maps?

Dorothy Westerman, the HR director, observed:

> 'I was working with a new management team, (dare I say, six gentlemen!) and myself their HR director. I recognised the need for development, as all of these guys had worked their way up and were technically competent but found the 'HR stuff' difficult. Working with Steve Jones, and using the Motivational Maps, initially there was some resistance; but they went with it, and I can absolutely say that for some of them it was a life changing exercise.
>
> For one individual, an important team member, the understanding of his motivational needs helped him to get things into perspective. He had previously often become very angry and frustrated in the work place. Before, the way he'd found of coping with the situation was through a regular visit for reflexology. Now that he understood his drivers and those of his colleagues, he became less quick to get angry; it really helped him to understand the other members of the team. He worked more collaboratively. It was a very distinct change for him and for others in the team; it enabled them to better understand why they behaved in the way they did. Just understanding yourself better can make all the difference.

Speaking personally, I myself have completed a new Motivational Map more recently having started a new job. I was bored, and thinking twice about staying. With my new management team, we completed the exercise. To my surprise my motivational needs had changed! Following this I was given more autonomy and a role in the team with a clearer direction. I noticed the change in myself, but it was actually very noticeable to others. It was like I had a new 'lease of life' someone commented.

I believe this process can help individuals, teams and as a result businesses to grow.

Dorothy Westerman

What was the impact of the maps?

The year-long programme proved to be very successful indeed. Not only did it achieve its objective of uniting the leadership team and board, but through the use of Motivational Maps it went even further.

In Lloyd Bates's, own words:

In the last year we have grown from £14.2 million turnover to £18.7, million, 30% growth, and this year we are on track to deliver £21.5 million turnover, another 15% growth. Our success is brought about by our people. We put a lot of effort into development about people and employee engagement, getting them to understand the journey we are on, our aspirations. You can put a plan in place, but without employee commitment you won't achieve it.

Lloyd Bates, MD

Lloyd highlighted that the vision and objectives had become clear, leadership were *clearer*, especially now leaders understood motivation and employee motivators, and this had led to much more regular communications via briefings and newsletters, and the deliberate intention of keeping everyone up-to-date with the progress on the journey. As a result of this, Aish Technologies scooped up a number of awards, including the Solent Business Award Winner 2016 for dynamic growth. This award highlights businesses demonstrating true growth and innovation with the energy and passion for delivering change, *while including ambition to develop their workforce to maximise technological, commercial and merger & aquisition opportunities.* Aish Technologies also won the Lloyds Bank small to medium-sized business of the year finalist 2017 award. This celebrated the contributions of small- and medium-sized enterprises to the UK economy, and recognised those businesses who have maintained a consistent growth and strong financial performance, understood their customers, *and who had an engaged workforce with effective leadership, with continual innovation to support future growth.*

Figure 9.6 Aish senior board celebrate with Steve Jones (back row, centre)

Creating the engaged workforce and effective leadership were critical to their success. But over and above winning awards, achieving public recognition, increasing turnover and profitability (Figure 9.6), goes one simple fact: the people – both leaders and employees – are happier, more satisfied, and the quality of their lives dramatically improved as a result of such initiatives.

Notes

1 In the first book in this series, James Sale, *Mapping Motivation*, Routledge (2016), the two case studies were corporate organisations; in the second book, James Sale and Bevis Moynan, *Mapping Motivation for Coaching*, Routledge (2018), the focus was on individual case studies; for this third book we have chosen small to medium-sized enterprises (SMEs), which in the UK is usually defined as companies employing up to 250 employees.
2 The next book in this series is *Mapping Motivation for Leadership*, James Sale and Jane Thomas, Routledge (2019), which expands greatly on the ideas in this volume.
3 James Sale and Bevis Moynan, op. cit.
4 FGH is a real but anonymised case study. Andrew Shaw who undertook the project currently works with Magenta Coaching Solutions, a senior Motivational Maps company.

5 Via Bevis Moynan, a leading Mapping coach, of Magenta Coaching Solutions, https://bit.ly/2GdRGXr.
6 The reference to incorporating Motivational Maps with a performance appraisal system is the whole topic of the forthcoming book from James Sale and Steve Jones, *Mapping Motivation for Appraisal*, Routledge (2020).
7 So, actually double the standard programme suggested in Figures 9.2 and 9.4. This re-emphasises the point that one size does not fit all. It is equally and entirely possible to 'halve' the standard input time for certain organisations. It will always depend on context and particular circumstances.

Conclusion

We began by saying that it was time for a change; the twentieth century has now gone, and as it has passed so its management models too have become outdated, outmoded and – worst of all – ineffective. Or, as governments like to say: no longer fit for purpose. In a new century we have new issues, new values, new priorities and one of these is people: people are important, people need to be valued, and to show it *and* to do it we need employee engagement strategies (and tactics as well). This book is full of just such strategies and tactics, and before we review them, let's be clear. This shift that has occurred is not mere altruism, or do-goodism, or hippy-dom writ large: there are clear commercial and value benefits attaching to organisations that seek to engage their employees; but, also, there are wellness benefits for the staff too. In short, the mission we are inviting all employers to embark upon is to increase the amount of wellness in the world at the same time as increasing their profits! Win–win.

The primary reason for engaging employees is to obtain that discretionary effort that they can choose to withhold. And when they choose to withhold it, then it is clear that they are not motivated by their work, their environment or their organisation, or all three. Motivation is the key to opening the lock of engagement, and we hope we have demonstrated this time and again throughout this book. In particular, we think that the Motivational Map profile and its associated team and organisational versions are ideal for this purpose, and that at long last we have a tool that can provide a language and metrics to give specificity to this (what has always been heretofore) most nebulous of topics. We can know how staff are feeling about their work and the organisation, and how engaged they are, not by the direct approach of a staff survey which we have given many reasons for suspecting (in Chapter 4), but through the indirect approach of Motivational Mapping.

And we have covered a lot of ground in these nine chapters: barriers that prevent engagement, and ways of re-framing them; understanding the seminal UK MacLeod Report on engagement and what it is, what the four enablers are and how Motivational Maps tap into them; creating a performance focus for engagement and using communication strategies to improve relationships at work; how Motivational Maps can help give employees a voice, and the need for managers to balance challenge and support; developing and supporting the necessary skills of the engaging manager and using Maps for two critical tasks of 360° feedback and recruitment; and how Motivational Maps tap into the strategic narrative of an organisation and which seven key metrics measure engagement indirectly. And, too, we have considered how integrity, motivation and engagement are related in some not obvious ways, as well as developing four key and necessary mind-sets for dealing with change. That is an awful lot of material, and most chapters contain at least seven activities to help the reader understand and implement the ideas.

Finally, we have carefully chosen three case studies in the small- to medium-sized enterprises (SME) category because it is there[1] that there is much neglect of this topic, and where as well managing directors and bosses feel that this 'academic' subject is either not for them, or that they don't have the resources of a corporate (often meaning: that's too expensive, isn't it?) to implement a programme. It should be clear from the studies that this is far from the truth: the benefits far outweigh the costs.

But we are entirely pragmatic, as opposed to being ideological, about this.[2] Yes, employee engagement as we've said is a strategic issue; it is a matter for the whole organisation to deliberate on and get behind implementing. Yet, we realise too that that can be too big a stretch for some, and so this book provides lots of tactics and techniques along the way that can help. It might be what we call a kaisen[3] approach – small incremental changes in the right direction, over time, can make a big difference. We said early on – in Chapter 2 in fact – that whilst all the four enablers were vital, and also interconnected in quite profound ways, if there were only one we focused on it would be the creation of the engaging manager. And this is because we know in the real world that organisations that have barely scratched the surface of employee engagement, may yet be organisations with high levels of staff engagement simply because they have spent a lot of time thinking about, recruiting, training and developing first rate managers – engaging managers in our sense of the words – and this creates results.

Perhaps it would be best to conclude this book with some thoughts from probably the best thinker on the future of management currently in the world: Gary Hamel[4] and his brilliant book, named appropriately, *The Future of Management*. Hamel observed, as we have been observing, that 'You can't solve new or chronic problems with fossilised principles'. In other words, with what we call the top-down approach. Furthermore, 'the redistribution of power is one of the primary means of making organisations more adaptable, more innovative, and more highly engaging.' This is what we are arguing for, what employee engagement demands: a bottom-up approach, starting with each employee's motivators. What do employees want? Let's solve that chronic problem, for if we do the employees will give us that extra discretionary effort and become engaged. This will achieve – what, exactly? 'Trust me, your employees are exercising their creativity *somewhere*, it just may not be at work', Hamel goes on to say. It will unleash their productivity. And critically, Hamel reminds and reassures us: 'The important issue here is the overall principle: management innovation is too important to be left to the experts.' Put more simply: we can do it! In reading this book you have a toolkit, a smorgasbord of ideas and techniques to enable you, as a manager, to begin that process of engaging employees wherever you work.

Finally, then, 'We often talk of goals, which are the objectives we keep in our head; but our motivations are the goals we actually want in our heart, and these we need to be far more expressive and clear about.'[5] Mapping Motivation is the way forward in this enterprise: we have over 40,000 Maps completed, by well over 400 practitioners in 14 countries, and a face validity rating of 95%; this tool can seriously get you into the hearts, not just the minds, of the employees and managers that you wish to engage.

We wish you well on your engagement journey and especially should you wish to make Mapping Motivation a core part of it.

Notes

1 The first book in the series, James Sale, *Mapping Motivation*, Gower (2016), actually had two corporate case studies, whereas the sequel, *Mapping Motivation for Coaching*, James Sale and Bevis Moynan, Routledge (2018), contained numerous individual case studies (as befitted the coaching process). Future books in the series will extend the range to include public and voluntary sector case studies.

2 Although we make it clear in Chapter 8 that 'interventions' – or purely tactical methods – are not sufficient in the long run to effect permanent change. But for various reasons – including experimentation, or dipping one's toe in the water first – people leading organisations may initially be resistant to commit. As Gary Hamel observes: 'It would seem that many managers have resigned themselves to the sub-optimal trade-offs and organisational incompetencies that are the inevitable side-effects of our early-20th-century management model.'

3 See Chapter 7 for more on kaisen.

4 Gary Hamel, *The Future of Management*, Harvard Business School Press (2007).

5 Kenneth W. Thomas, *Intrinsic Motivation at Work*, Barrett-Koehler (2009).

Resources

This section of the book is designed to help you find more information about motivation, engagement and Motivational Maps. It is not comprehensive and will be subsequently updated.

Information about Motivation Maps Ltd and Motivational Maps

Motivational Maps Ltd was founded in 2006. It is ISO accredited: ISO 17065: www.irqao.com/PDF/C11364-51147.pdf.

The company website can be found at www.motivationalmaps.com and enquiries should be addressed to info@motivationalmaps.com.

James Sale, the author, can be found at www.jamessale.co.uk, Dorset, and his LinkedIn profile is: https://uk.linkedin.com/in/jamesmotivationsale.

Steve Jones, the co-author, can be found at: www.skillsforbusinesstraining.co.uk, Hampshire, UK. His LinkedIn profile is: https://uk.linkedin.com/in/stevejonesmotivation.

For more information on how to become an accredited Mapping Motivation for Engagement consultant contact Steve Jones at steve@skillsforbusinesstraining.co.uk.

There are currently four different Motivational Maps available, and this book explores some aspects of three of them:

1. The Motivational Map is for individuals and employees to discover what motivates them and how motivated they are; this produces a 15-page report on the individual.
2. The Motivational Team Map, which the forthcoming book, *Mapping Motivation for Management* (Routledge, 2019) is largely devoted to. This is a 22+-page report which synthesises the individual maps from any number of people, and reveals what the overall motivational scores are. It is ideal for team leaders and managers.
3. The Motivational Organisational Map produces a 44-page report and synthesises the information from any number of team maps be they

from the whole organisation or a section of the whole organisation. It is ideal for senior managers to understand how to implement their strategies through people. In 2020, Routledge will release *Mapping Motivation for Strategy and Change*, which will cover aspects of this diagnostic.

4. The Motivational Youth Map is different from the other Maps in that it has three outputs: one for the student, one for the teacher and one for the parent; all designed to help motivate the student to succeed at school and college. It is ideal for 11–18 year olds and schools and colleges looking to motivate their students. There is also the Youth Group Map.

The Motivational Map questionnaire is in nine different languages: English, German, French, Italian, Greek, Lithuanian, Spanish, Hungarian and Portuguese.
Motivational Maps Ltd has licensed over 400 consultants, coaches and trainers to deliver the Map products in 14 countries. There are five senior practitioners of Maps in the UK:

UK senior practitioners

Bevis Moynan, Magenta Coaching Solutions, www.magentac.co.uk, Cambridgeshire

Carole Gaskell, Full Potential Group, www.fullpotentialgroup.co.uk, London

Jane Thomas, Premier Life Skills, www.premierlifeskills.co.uk, Dorset

Kate Turner, Motivational Leadership, www.motivationalleadership.co.uk, Wiltshire

Susannah Brade-Waring, Aspirin Business Solutions, www.aspirinbusiness.com, Dorset

There is one international senior practitioner of Maps:

Akeela Davies, Courageous Business Culture, www.courageousbusinessculture.com, Canada

Motivational Maps Resources can be found on www.motivationalmaps.com/resources

Other key books on motivation, engagement and personal development

Nine books we like on motivation, engagement, and related topics are:

The Employee Experience Advantage, Jacob Morgan, Wiley (2017).
Full Engagement, Brian Tracy, American Management Association (2011).
The Future of Management, Gary Hamel, Harvard Business School Press (2007).
The High Engagement Work Culture, David Bowles and Cary Cooper, Palgrave Macmillan (2012).

Intrinsic Motivation at Work, Kenneth W. Thomas, Barrett-Koehler (2009).
Motivation for Creative People, Mark McGuiness, Lateral Action Books (2015).
The Oxford Handbook of Work Engagement, Motivation and Self-Determination Theory, edited Marylène Gagnè, Oxford University Press (2014).
Start with Why, Simon Sinek, Portfolio Penguin (2009).
Winning the Story Wars, Jonah Sachs, Harvard Business Review Press (2012).

Index

Westerman, Dorothy 165–7
willpower 10
win-win 16, 98, 170
wisdom 19, 48
workers 1, 7, 77, 80, 124, 130
workplace 11, 15, 31, 88, 116, 130
World War 2 130
world-class 123, 125, 165
wrapping 11

writers 5, 15
wrong 10, 13, 18–19, 57, 96, 98, 114, 132,
  134, 136–7, 142, 145, 157

yang 44
Yeats, W. B. 47
yin 44

zone 20–1, 23–4, 31, 40, 78, 115, 143

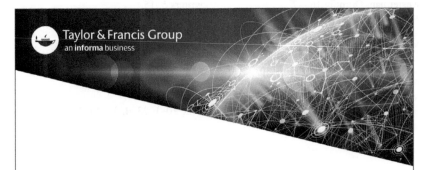